The Transformation of Desire

The Transformation of Desire

How Desire Became Corrupted –
and How We Can Reclaim It

DIARMUID O'MURCHU MSC

ORBIS BOOKS
Maryknoll, New York 10545

Founded in 1970, Orbis Books endeavors to publish works that enlighten the mind, nourish the spirit, and challenge the conscience. The publishing arm of the Maryknoll Fathers and Brothers, Orbis seeks to explore the global dimensions of the Christian faith and mission, to invite dialogue with diverse cultures and religious traditions, and to serve the cause of reconciliation and peace. The books published reflect the views of their authors and do not represent the official position of the Maryknoll Society. To learn more about Maryknoll and Orbis Books, please visit our website at www.maryknoll.org.

First published in Great Britain in 2007 by
Darton, Longman and Todd Ltd
1 Spencer Court
140-142 Wandsworth High Street
London SW18 4JJ
Great Britain

First published in the USA in 2007 by
Orbis Books
P.O. Box 308
Maryknoll, New York 10545-0308
U.S.A.

Printed and bound in Great Britain.

Library of Congress Cataloging-in-Publication Data

Ó Murchú, Diarmuid.
   The transformation of desire : how desire became corrupted and how we can reclaim it / Diarmuid O'Murchu.
      p. cm.
   ISBN 978-1-57075-704-4 (pbk.)
   1. Christianity and culture. 2. Desire—Religious aspects—Christianity. 3. Consumption (Economics)—Religious aspects—Christianity. I. Title.
   BR115.C8O23 2007
   241—dc22

                          2006034095

Contents

Introduction

Books have been among my best companions on the journey of life, not just as an author but particularly as a reader. Books come my way often from strange and unexpected sources, and every now and again books befriend me in ways I had not even remotely envisaged. The connection certainly has a synchronistic feel to it.

Several years ago, I was one of four men and about twenty women gathered in a church in London, UK for the Ash Wednesday distribution of ashes. As the young priest dispensed the ashes to each person, he used the old formula: 'Remember, O man, thou art but dust and unto dust shalt thou return.' Had the congregation been predominantly made up of men, then there might be some logic to this choice of words, but to experience the sexist words being addressed to each woman left me feeling both sad and angry.

The experience was even more disturbing in the light of what I was reading around that time. The scientific community was beginning to explore the significance of the creative vacuum, in which dust is portrayed as being infused with sub-atomic particles all of which are believed to be alive. The more I read about it, the more it set my soul and intellect on fire. But, obviously, the priest distributing the ashes shared neither my wisdom nor exhilaration.

On my way home, I passed by one of London's big bookstores and with some time to spare I decided to pop in and browse around. Just inside the door, on display were six of the store's most recent acquisitions, and staring me in the eyes in large blue print were the words: VITAL DUST! It was the recently published work of Christian de Duve, covering his research on the nature of dust for which he had won the Nobel Prize. Within the space of one hour I had crossed over from the world of insipid religiosity to the inspiring world of scientific exploration. Another synchronistic moment in which a book came to nourish my deep desires.

*

The present work is inspired by a much more recent book: *Liberation Theology and the End of History* by Daniel Bell. The title is somewhat misleading. The book is really about human desire and the corrosive impact of contemporary globalisation on the desires of the human heart. Contemporary market forces augmented by seductive advertising have consumed the human spirit, awakening a vast range of insatiable desires for allurements that become more and more irresistible. Addictive cravings have consumed our capacity for desire, leaving millions in our world starved for a false fulfilment that eats ever more voraciously into the human psyche.

Bell offers a penetrating analysis of this subtle but highly seductive force of our time. To resolve the dilemma, he invokes the call to justice as the perennial challenge now facing the human species. So many of the relationships between person and planet, as well as between human and human, are postulated on premises that are not merely false, but highly destructive. And the destruction undermines not just the fabric of social and political life, but indeed the deepest yearnings and hopes of the human heart.

*

Picking up Bell's suggestion that the human capacity for desire is being subverted by cultural forces of our time, I want to reclaim what that desire is about in its deepest meaning, a task attempted by other contemporary writers such as Conlon (2004), Eldredge (2000), Farley (2005), Grey (2003) and Zweig (2003). Science explains all our desires in terms of genetic forces seeking the survival of their own genes, while religion seeks to eliminate desire as the primary cause of sin, temptation and suffering in our world. Both science and religion seem unable to grasp the deeper meaning of human desiring.

The longings of the human heart, the desires for meaning, purpose and fulfilment are all born of a yearning that defies rational explanation. Mystics have known this for many millennia. And so have most humans, if they could learn to trust their intuitive wisdom. But our educational systems have effectively indoctrinated us to be subservient consumers, who don't ask informed questions and collude with those who claim they can satiate our essential hungers. Millions are growing angry and disillusioned; the façade cannot be tolerated much longer.

This book is for all those who want to reclaim their intuitive wisdom and outgrow the propaganda that has controlled our lives and our hearts for far too long. It is a book that seeks to engender hope and vitality beyond the several destructive forces that engulf our world today. The human spirit was never meant to live with so much fear and helplessness. We need to reclaim the inner resources through which, once more, we can learn to live with integrity, meaning and joy in our daily lives.

PART ONE

The Corruption of Desire

If we are to avoid the catastrophes that loom on the horizon, rethinking our desires is exactly what we must do.

Gil Bailie (1997)

1

When Desire Is Not Fulfilled

Much unhappiness in our time results from the fact that our deepest desires are neither met nor fulfilled.

> Beyond what is imagined by reason, there is something imagined by desire, poetry, beauty. This concept of the imagination bets on life without mathematical certitude; it bets simply because life is worth being loved and lived to the full.
>
> *Ivone Gebara (2002)*

Most people associate desire with happiness in life. We desire to be happy. And for most of us this involves having close friends, meaningful relationships, fulfilling work, a place called home, and an overall sense that life is worth living. Religious belief may add the assurance that many desires not fulfilled in this life will be realised in the next life. This conviction meant a great deal more in earlier times than it does today, and is likely to be embraced by older rather than younger people.

What we desire, and how we might satisfy those desires, seems reasonably clear – at least in theory. In practice, we are dealing with a complex phenomenon, affected by several cultural factors, some very ancient, like religion, others much more recent like advertising and the ways our desires are 'driven' today by marketing forces and the power of consumerism. Furthermore, there is the moralistic cultural tone of the word itself: for many people desire is over-identified with sex, for others with power, for others with possessions, and for some with the need to be in charge of one's life and destiny.

In this opening chapter, I outline our tendency to distort and even corrupt the human capacity for desire. As a species we are often alienated from the very desires that give meaning and purpose to our existence. I then outline the major challenges facing us if we are to reclaim and appropriate our desires in a more integrated and fulfilling way.

Distortions of desire

The following are some of the key obstacles to the realisation of our desires, which in Part One I suggest distort, and even corrupt, our very capacity for desiring. These include:

- an internalisation of religious values, which in the past tried to convince us that desire could only be satisfied after this life, and not during it, and often leaves us feeling guilty about desire and its fulfilment
- an over-identification of desire with sex, with sexuality often understood as a dangerous, instinctual drive, morally dubious and needing to be firmly controlled
- the consumption of desire through the lurid attractions of advertising and marketing forces in our time, often compelling us to purchase and own things far in excess of our needs
- the fierce culture of competition in which we are never satisfied with 'enough'! We feel we must be as good as everybody else and often seek power to outwit and dominate others
- political and economic disempowerment, through which people internalise a sense that they have no real say in the social or political spheres, nor do they see any meaningful way to make a contribution to life on a larger scale
- the lack of meaningful work, forced on millions in our world through unemployment. Yet, in several Western countries, regular employment leaves many people feeling victimised by exploitation and the under-use of their gifts and talents
- feelings of inadequacy and fear in a world growing progressively more violent, insecure and unsafe for humans.

Liberating authentic desire

In Parts Two and Three, I explore what desire might look like in a different context. Here I am striving to honour the deeper, spiritual nature of desire. Only then can we hope to rehabilitate desire in a more creative and integrated way in the ordinary realms of daily life. I make some bold and original claims, setting desire in a much larger context and exploring the re-appropriation of desire in a much more challenging and inspiring way.

The new context includes the following considerations:

- Desire is not merely a human propensity. Scientific developments of the past century, particularly the quantum theory in physics, alert us to a universe imbued with dynamic energy, suggesting that creation itself 'desires' to grow and flourish.
- We humans appropriate this cosmic sense of yearning through our groundedness in planet earth, which in evolutionary terms moves towards a greater realisation of its innate potential, a claim that is basic to the Gaia theory expounding the notion of the earth as an alive organism.
- Being at home in creation, and being able to engage creatively with it, seems an essential prerequisite for the articulation and realisation of human desire. Several important social, political and economic consequences arise – all of which I explore in Parts Two and Three.
- Spiritual dimensions play a central role in this expanded vision. The driving force that feeds the desire of creation may be a new way to understand the formative influence of the Holy Spirit, as explored by contemporary theologians like Denis Edwards (2004) and Mark Wallace (2005). I am not merely articulating a spirituality of desire; rather I am suggesting that desire itself is essentially spiritual in nature.
- Nor must we hastily glamorise these profound insights. The new cosmology informs us that creation thrives through the paradox of creation-and-destruction. Light and darkness forever intermingle. Desire can often be luminous and liberating, but it can also be insatiable and potentially destructive. Skills for discernment (Chapter 33) become crucial at this level.
- What we previously defined as personal desires, often understood in individual terms, now become not merely interpersonal, but also take on an interdependent significance. There is no such thing as a human desire in isolation. All our desiring belongs to an intentionality that is cosmic, planetary and spiritual in its true essence.
- Therefore the desire for happiness and fulfilment can only be realised in a world where the desires of creation are also honoured.

The practical implications of this claim require a radical rethinking of how we work for justice (Chapter 23).

• Prioritising human desire, especially in terms of privilege and rights, will need to be re-evaluated. The cultural historian Theodore Roszak articulated this concern several years ago when he wrote: 'The needs of the planet are the needs of the person ... the rights of the person are the rights of the planet' (1978: xxx).

Towards a new integration

My primary aim in this book is to help people integrate their desires in ways that will lead to greater happiness and fulfilment. Contrary to several utopias promised in our time, and several panaceas for the realisation of human potential, I am proposing a way forward that requires extensive reform of social and religious behaviours and the institutions that uphold those behaviours. And this is not merely a personal challenge; it is interpersonal in several important ways. It also embraces urgent ecological, political and planetary engagements for our time.

By seeking to transcend the narrow, functional parameters of daily experience I am not advocating escapism in any form. I am proposing a relocation for human meaning and fulfilment, a larger context that will honour reward as well as motivation and pleasure (cf. Schroeder 2004). Innate to our being and becoming are cosmic and planetary dimensions, spiritual and holistic aspects. As creatures of desire, we can only become whole when we honour the wholeness of our God-given context. Then a more enduring and authentic form of happiness becomes possible.

2

What About the Phenomenology of Desire?

Philosophers analyse desire in a very cerebral way and miss the deeper psychic and spiritual meaning.

Currently, psychologists are considered to be the 'experts' in analysing desire, but those of a more rationalistic persuasion prefer the analysis offered by philosophers, particularly those known as phenomenologists. I offer a brief overview of the leading ideas.

Freud heavily identifies desire with instinct and, for Freud, instinct is always questionable, and frequently dangerous. Freudian instinct has a kind of will of its own, invoking intense passion and feeling and driving the human to act in ways that are a threat to reason and rationality. Carl Jung challenged the Freudian view, offering an alternative interpretation of desire that incorporated many insights from the great mystical traditions. But because rationalism is so deeply ingrained in the Western psyche and in the scholarly world, Jung has never gained the popularity or distinction attributed to Freud.

Analysing desire

Meanwhile, Freud's key concepts were refined and in the process redefined. Freudian psychoanalysis came to be understood not so much as a process for bringing subconscious material to conscious awareness, but more as a study of desire itself (see Fuery 1995: 8).

Jacques Lacan is a leading name in this endeavour, with valuable contributions from other French theorists such as Gilles Deleuze, Jacques Derrida and Michel Foucault. French feminists Hélène Cixous, Luce Irigaray and Julia Kristeva embrace a similar psycho-analytical perspective, keeping the focus of attention more on female desire and its subversion within phallo-centric culture.

Lacan distinguishes between *desire, need* and *demand*. Whereas need and demand can be tied to specific objects and relations, desire always exceeds those objects and the subject's relationship to them. Lacan describes four main features of desire: subjectivity, significa-tion, cultural production and the analytical processes:

Subjectivity: It is in the process of negotiating my desires that I come to a sense of personal identity. My desires are not drives or instincts to be subdued or eliminated, but creative urges that need to be embraced and integrated.

Signification: My desires are always focused on an Other (the signifier), and most of the time I am not consciously aware of this. I am always desiring something I have not got. It may be an object, a person, a dream. The object of my desire is never fully attained and so I go on desiring more. Inevitably this leaves me feeling unfulfilled and incomplete – what Lacan calls a split-subject, at the mercy of Girard's mimetic rivalry. So for Lacan, 'the act of desire is both an essential part of being and a process that also jeopardises the sense of existence' (Fuery 1995: 24).

Cultural production: To negotiate our desires and the entire human culture characterised primarily by desire, we produce structures of communication such as language, religions and institutions. Of particular interest to Lacan, and to many post-modernists of our time, is our use of language mediated through various *texts*. In this regard, text is not just the written word: it includes the entire repertoire of story, language, communication and artistic expression, through which we try to read reality and communi-cate with it.

Analytical processes: According to Julia Kristeva, desire is part of the signifying process but, because desire is never totally fulfilled, it does not simply merge with signification; rather, it alters the object of desire. The process of psychoanalysis facilitates a bet-ter understanding of our desire to connect, the risk of projecting, and the ongoing task of relating more meaningfully.

> Desire has been figured as a slippage, as the alterity of the social
> order, as beyond satisfaction and quite without resolution, as an
> essential constituent in the formulation of subjectivity, and as a site
> of power and control beyond the law which sustains such sites ...
> Desire is in itself extremely complex.
>
> *Patrick Fuery (1995)*

Inherently ambiguous

Those who try to understand desire from a phenomenological angle
broadly agree on the following dynamics of desire:

- *Desire is inescapable.* It seems to be a core element in the will-to-
  life. It is the 'something more' that we wish to attain; while
  rational reason informs us that these attainments cannot be
  reached, or at best can only be reached in a good-enough way,
  something deep within the psyche urges us to keep pursuing, and
  to maintain the pursuit with intensity. It is our desiring that keeps
  us focused on transcendent meaning.
- *Desire is full of ambiguity.* It embraces a potentiality we deeply
  yearn for but one that we can never fully attain. And each new
  attainment awakens other desires. Restlessness of spirit is
  inevitable, interpreted by religion as a yearning for God (or God's
  love) which can only be realised after death in the life of eternal
  bliss.
- *Desire for the greater part is a subconscious process.* We can negotiate
  its demands with greater ease when it becomes conscious. There
  are many ways we can do this, and not just through psycho-
  analytical or psychotherapeutic programmes. More importantly,
  however, is the wisdom to recognise the subconscious or partially
  hidden dimensions of our desiring. I wish to emphasise this point,
  because no matter what strategies we use – psychological, spiritual or cultural – we can never be totally aware of our desiring; if,
  indeed, we were ever to become totally aware, we would be so
  overwhelmed, human survival would probably be impossible.
- *Honouring desire requires deep wisdom.* While the psychological and
  philosophical literature places the emphasis on the splits, slip-
  pages, failures and frustrations of unattained desire, as a species
  we seem reluctant to face the paradoxical truth of our capacity for
  desire. *This is a gift to be embraced rather than a malady to be got rid of*
  or, alternatively, a primeval curse we grudgingly must live with.

Our desire is not about sin or temptation, but about yearning, longing, fulfilment, purpose. We need a deeper wisdom to accommodate, appropriate and embrace desire in a new way.

Striving for the ineffable

The more we try to rationalise the phenomenon of desire, the more it eludes our analysis. Desire, it seems, has something to do with what Paul Ricoeur calls *the surplus of meaning*. Its object is unattainable, because we are reaching for the ineffable, and we do this because it is in our nature to do so. No matter how abhorrent it may seem to contemporary rational thought and discourse, we humans are programmed for mystery, and that ultimately is the goal of all our desiring.

> Desire does not wait until we are free from illusion or anger. Desire itself will guide us, past, and through all our mistakes, pain, losses, and moments of despair. If we can connect with even the smallest hint of this desire, which emanates from the divine image deep within us, then nothing, not even ourselves, can break this thread that leads us home.
>
> *Wendy Farley (2005)*

The phenomenologists seem to regard desire as a distinctive human characteristic. Their terms of reference are quite anthropocentric and, inevitably, reductionistic. They focus very much on the here-and-now, largely bypassing transcendent or teleological features. Some see desire as one more brain-process to be investigated by neuro-science (cf. Schroeder 2004). In the present work I wish to highlight the *teleology*, the goal(s) which inform our desiring at every stage of its being and becoming. And these goals are primarily cosmic, planetary and transpersonal, as I indicate in Part Two of this book.

3

Desire: A Confused Landscape

Both internal and external influences undermine an authentic understanding of what desire means.

Fidelity to external codes often dictates the way in which we engage with reality, including our appropriation of religion. We judge ourselves and each other by external performance, frequently by how well we can 'sell' ourselves, our talents, our bodies and the material goods that make money. Faced with such spiritual and cultural dislocation, we scarcely need a spiritually informed writer like John O'Donohue (1997: 14) to remind us that 'If we become addicted to the external, our interiority will haunt us.'

The inner sense of being haunted is constructed on a double alienation:

1. Desire finds its home in our inner being. However, with so much emphasis on external achievement, and everything evaluated in terms of its commercial value, the capacity for desire has been infiltrated by external rather than internal sustenance. Inner pain, expressed as loneliness, alienation, emptiness, confusion, depression, is swamping the human psyche at an alarming rate. The drug culture reaps the benefits as millions seek to block out or suppress their pain. Many people are confused, largely because they do not understand the real meaning of desire.

2. While the external world emphasises reason and rational discourse, paradoxically, the commercial world capitalises on primal instinct, using incredibly sophisticated advertising to saturate the human psyche with addictive desire. We end up with a double addiction: externally, to the rationalism and legalism that

characterise the public forums of modern society (elucidated by Plumwood 2002) and, internally, to the inflated passions for purchasing and possessing so many things that we really don't need at all.

Humans tend not to entertain inner alienation for too long. It becomes too painful, intolerable. Now that religion is failing to tend the inner soul, we re-invent the wheel with a vast range of spiritual buffers. *Spirituality* has become the new panacea, but often offering 'fixes' of no enduring value (see Grey 2003: 152ff.). It has infiltrated the psychological and social sciences, and it exerts a widespread appeal in the business world today (cf. Carrette and King 2005).

Religion and alienation

> Modern Christianity could be characterised as obsessed with desire. Modern Christianity is obsessed with subduing desire, with controlling desire, understood as the natural passions and reactions of the body to external stimuli. Far from leaving desire behind, modern Christianity seeks to subdue and bring it before the bar of reason.
>
> *Daniel Bell (2001)*

Why did something as noble and inspiring as religion become the basis for so much conflict with the desires of our hearts? In part, the answer rests with a distrust of human nature that seems to have infiltrated all the major religions. In Christian faith it is called *a fundamental flaw*, and in theological terms described as *Original Sin*. The Christian version goes like this: there was a rebellion in the heavenly realm where the sky God reigns supreme. The rebellious angels were ousted and fell to earth. They became the propagators of a new species, called humans. Inevitably, humans were flawed from the beginning. The flaw has variously been named, with Original Sin being one of the most enduring labels.

It is intriguing that humans have taken this preposterous myth so seriously. Even where religion no longer commands strong allegiance, it tends to prevail, generating a sense of pessimism, despair and alienation. Human desiring is at best defective and, therefore, often held in suspicion. In our capacity for desire, the defectiveness of the fallen angels continues to haunt us. Not alone is our desiring corrupt, but it seems to be endowed with a power for spreading corruption, and only the intervening power of God's redemption can save us from the contaminating influence.

> Rather than rebellion against God being the primary sin that engenders all others, I see rebellion against creation as the fundamental sin.
>
> *Marjorie H. Suchocki (1999)*

Institutionalising desire

In this anthropocentric ideology, humans are all important. Man is the measure of all things! That being the case, everything in creation is for human usufruct, and must be considered inferior to the human. And the human begins to assume a sense of controlling power, channelling desire into what some phenomenologists call *controlling enclosures*. Daniel Bell (2001: 31ff.) observes:

> At the heart of disciplinary society was the closed space, the enclosure. The disciplined, docile body was formed by being channelled through a series of enclosures – school, hospital, factory, army, prison – where it was moulded in accord with a norm. Currently, these enclosures are in crisis.

As a species we are emerging from a protracted period in which the containment and conformity of desire was channelled through a number of standardised institutions. In this culture of control, desire was a subject of suspicion, a dimension of experience that could never be trusted, and rather than allow it scope for ventilation, it was incarcerated whenever and wherever possible.

According to the French philosopher Gilles Deleuze, the time frame of the closed disciplinary system is collapsing; the culture of patriarchal dominance is wearing thin; it has outlived its usefulness, but as yet nobody from within the major institutions dares to question its hegemony.

Meanwhile, open-ended systems invade the landscape. Access to information, through the computer, the web and several attempts to make public information more accessible, is a manifestation of this new amorphous freedom. Much more significant, although largely unacknowledged, is the extensive disillusionment with which people regard public institutions, especially political, religious

and economic ones. Amid the political sensationalism that characterises politics in the USA, few seem to see any need to confront the
massive apathy whereby a mere 50 per cent of the electorate
exercised the right to vote in the past six presidential elections. The
other 50 per cent could not muster the energy or good will to cast
the vote. Faith in the great and glamorous presidency of the
USA is nowhere as strong and coherent as the media would have us
believe.

With major institutions rapidly sinking into dysfunctionality, the
need for alternative social and political structures is already coming
to light. The most obvious alternative will be that of *networks*, groups
and organisations endowed with the fluidity and flexibility to
embrace and address authentic human desires. Proclaimed by the
United Nations in the 1970s, the networking principle (as in the
NGO – non-governmental organisation) has gained widespread
credibility, but is still battling for official recognition as patriarchal
institutions desperately cling to the old ways of doing things. (More
on this topic in Part Three.)

Resolving the confusion

As indicated in the opening chapter, only a major conceptual shift
can rescue us from the distortions of desire in which we are
entangled. People of our time are rapidly losing faith in major
institutions. Paradoxically, others, captivated by fear and insecurity,
are flocking to sects and cults where they are offered hyped-up
reassurances of no lasting value. We also detect in parts of the world
a shift to more right-wing governments, particularly noticeable in
the USA. These are all short-sighted strategies offering little long-
term hope for the fulfilment of human desire.

To endure the darkness and confusion of this time requires great
wisdom and unstinting hope. The chaos at times feels overwhelming, and this cultural disintegration will probably get worse before
getting better. It is a classical dark night of the soul, except in our
time taking place on a global scale. It is a time for focused energies
and a great deal of discerning wisdom (see Moore 2004).

It is also a time when many people are thrown back on their
individual resources. To go against the grain, think differently and
act alternatively, takes enormous courage and resilience. And while
requiring individual strength of character, few of us are likely to
sustain the endeavour without the support of kindred spirits.

Fortunately, such support groups seem to be flourishing, many using the Internet as the initial point of contact.

And hopefully the wisdom of these pages, depressing and disturbing though it may be (especially in Part One), will help to clarify the confused landscape, demarcating what is dying and no longer useful, and opening up alternative possibilities that proffer a more promising future.

4

Desire Eternally Postponed

Postponing the fulfilment of desire to an afterlife is no longer meaningful.

Human beings desire many things, ranging from personal needs we feel each day to the desire for a better existence on earth. Today, a variety of different sciences explore the meaning and articulation of our desiring. For several centuries, however, the understanding was confined to one science, namely *religion*. While acknowledging the actual existence of desire, religion tends to encourage disengagement from desire, postulating that its fulfilment belongs to the next life rather than this one.

God alone can satisfy our desires, and most of them can only be fulfilled after this life. Hence the popularity of St Augustine's words: 'You have made us for yourself, O God, and our hearts are restless 'til they rest with you' (*Confessions*, Book 1.1). Here Augustine states two central convictions: firstly, God alone can satisfy our desires and, secondly, that being the case, we are condemned to life-long restlessness till we obtain fulfilment in eternal life.

All the major religions have much to say about desire, but most of it is about bringing it under the bar of reason, *controlling* desire as an unruly passion, best kept under the thumb of vigilance, prayer and penance. For all the religions, desire, at best, is suspect, with God often perceived as 'the divine thwarter' (Eldredge 2000: 89).

Religion has actually prevented us from coming to terms with desire in its deep meaning, and, therefore, has left us with a legacy of confusion, emptiness, guilt, fear and restlessness, all of which are encapsulated in the metaphor of *exile*, a recurring theme in the literature of spirituality (more on this topic in Chapters 25 and 26; for a more extensive treatment, see O'Murchu 2000).

Living with postponement

> The patriarchal order is based upon worlds of the beyond: worlds of before birth and especially the after-life, other planets to be discovered and exploited for survival, etc. It doesn't appreciate the real value of the world we have and draws upon its often bankrupt blueprints on the basis of hypothetical worlds.
>
> *Luce Irigaray (1987)*

Whether it is the desire for peace, happiness, fulfilment or a better future, from a religious point of view, we are always kept waiting! Time and again, the spiritual traditions warn us that we should not invest too heavily in our desiring; we could be disappointed, but worse still it could spell spiritual and moral ruination for our immortal souls.

In religious terms, false desire – and for religion most desiring is false – haunts our existence from the cradle to the grave. There are so many things we desire, even on a daily basis. And those desires so easily can become cravings, addictions, compulsions, gross distractions from the religious path which alone can lead to happiness and fulfilment.

Desiring is infiltrated with uncertainty, ambiguity, angst. It is always a challenge for our spiritual equanimity. Monastic people sought to channel its impact by fleeing the world in favour of the monastery and hermitage. Yet, the spiritual records indicate all too clearly that this is not always a remedy for the urgings of desire. In fact, in several cases it seems to have intensified the yearnings of the human heart.

The dualistic world view

Several of the great spiritual traditions encourage devotees to adopt a meditation practice,[1] through which we calm down sensations, focus on the here and now, and keep our minds clear of the thoughts and feelings that distract from the things of God. Several of these approaches, whether intended or not, seem to arise from a dualistic world view, in which immersion in the world and its affairs is somewhat alien from God, and the choice to transcend the pre-occupation with the world is deemed to be more congruent with an authentic spiritual life.

Only in the past few decades have we acknowledged the distinctive influence of classical Greek culture (especially after Plato) on our ways of understanding spirituality, particularly the adoption of the dualistic world view. This is the kernel of the alienation through which we experience our desiring as something dangerous and problematic. The tendency to divide life, and especially spirituality, into binary opposing values (for example, sacred versus secular) is a relatively recent development in the spiritual story of the human species, and one that awaits thorough re-examination. Juxtaposing reality in terms of binary opposites is not innate to many ancient cultures of the Far East and, as Neil Douglas-Klotz (1999) indicates, has little place in either the Aramaic or Hebrew world views.

One of the reasons why we are reluctant to submit such spirituality to closer scrutiny is the claim that many saints and holy people have been produced through this system. Obviously it is scary to look too closely or critically, because the edifice upon which we have built our sanctity and sanity might begin to look precarious, and might begin to feel shaky.

Reclaiming spirituality

A good deal of the confusion I alluded to in Chapter 3 above belongs to this realm, particularly the crucial distinction between religion and spirituality. There is a widespread assumption that religion comes first and spirituality follows later. Even a limited acquaintance with culture and history will indicate that the opposite is often the case.

Humans have been behaving in a spiritual manner for thousands, perhaps millions, of years. Formal religion as we know it today is less than 5,000 years old. Equipped with spiritual endowment, and using it creatively over several thousands of years (it seems), we humans engaged our desires in a spiritually informed and, dare I suggest, spiritually enlightened way. Spirituality can handle desiring much more effectively and dynamically than religion.

> The moralistic insistence that we desire only God and eternal life can be quite unhelpful. It tends to carry a misleading interpretation of our nature and our desire. It is also a terrible distortion of the

sacred and holy mystery that dwells beyond being and pervades all that is.

Wendy Farley (2005)

In a previous work, I describe the revitalisation of spirituality in contemporary cultures. This is an exciting field, and not without its critics. While researchers like Dreyer and Burrows (2005), Forman (2004), Tacey (2004) and Flanagan and Kelly (2004) describe the new movements in spirituality in a positively affirming way, Carrette and King (2005) issue a blistering attack. They claim that spirituality feeds our consumerist culture with a false utopia. Spirituality today is the generic label for a whole range of 'new age' products (commodities), deviously marketed to pacify the privatised individualism of corporate capitalism. Spirituality, they argue, has been bought out by the corporate market forces of our time and is used to usurp the power of religion to transmit more enduring values: 'Spirituality has become the primary means facilitating the corporate take-over of religion' (Carrette & King 2005: 123).

The critique of Carrette and King is informed and timely, but misguided in its portrayal of religion. It seems to me that it is the failure of religion to nourish and sustain authentic spirituality that has begotten the new flurry of spiritual technologies, which, admittedly, are in danger of being corrupted by corporate and consumerist interests. Religion has monopolised the control of truth and liberation, setting up a new hegemony (an ultimate truth) which fails to speak meaningfully to millions of people in our time, leaving many spiritually parched, and thus hungering for a meaningful alternative.

Spirituality has become the alternative, and as typically happens in times of major transition, it is veering towards an opposite extreme. While religion maintained a semblance of conformity, spirituality today embraces huge diversity. While religion adopted institutions, spirituality opts for very loose and flexible structures. While religion prioritised divinely informed power as the basis of all truth, spirituality seeks to empower from the base up. Spirituality is replacing religion, not usurping it as Carrette and King (2005) suggest.

Neglected elements

Religion has reaped much of its own destruction precisely because it tried to control desire and prevent humans from appropriating desire in a more congruent way. And in its conventional scriptures and structures, it is unable to engage the contemporary world in a meaningful dialogue, particularly around some significant discoveries of modern science, e.g., insights from neuro-science indicating that our brains are programmed to desire reward and fulfilment (Schroeder 2004).

Spirituality, on the other hand, runs a distinctive danger of over-indulging desire – the delusion Carrette and King (2005) name so coherently – but failing to delineate its purpose and role in human becoming. Desire is structured on powerful subliminal forces. Cosmic and planetary dimensions inform all our primal longings (see Part Two). Archetypal energies abound in all our desiring.

Transpersonal drives push open horizons that neither current education nor conventional religion is capable of understanding. We are not trained to engage desire in a constructive or creative way. These subliminal, archetypal, neglected dimensions will be reclaimed, and examined more thoroughly, in subsequent chapters of this book. I now wish to review briefly other features of contemporary life through which we strive to channel our desiring, highlighting the corrupting influences of these misguided strategies.

5

Desire and the Preoccupation with Sex

Desire has been over-identified with the sex drive, and this has distorted its deeper meaning.

A cursory glance at the 5,800 allusions to desire in the research web-page www.highbeam.com illustrates all too vividly the eroticisation of desire in the contemporary world. At least 80 per cent of the references are about sexual desire and in most cases they allude to frustrated and unfulfilled desire. Desire is a sexual problem, a compulsive drive, an unruly instinct. Desire is categorically framed as a problematic area, one that haunts the human mind and disturbs the human spirit.

The nature of desire has been corrupted by over-identifying sex and desire. The literature on sexual desire tends to problematise our desiring, suggesting time and again that sex is something wild and destructive that needs to be tamed and controlled. And when we cannot subject it to such control, it is often suggested that sin and immorality have taken hold of our lives; or we are the unfortunate victims of a vast range of sexual addictions that characterise our time.

What is sexuality?

It seems to me that we are entangled in a problem of our own making. We have defined human sexuality, and appropriated a culture of sexual decorum, that no longer makes sense, because, in fact, it never did make sense. It is the breakdown of this dysfunctional model that leads to so much sexualised confusion today.

Nearly all historical accounts of human sexuality begin with the Greeks, dating the rise of human sexuality to some 2,500 years ago. The writings of Plato and Aristotle seem to be particularly important. Why? Presumably because that is where scholars tend to begin academic exploration on several topics of concern to human beings.

The short-sightedness of this approach should be obvious. If we begin with the Greeks of 2,500 years ago, then we are choosing to ignore over 99 per cent of our story and experience as a human species. We have inhabited the earth for an estimated *six million years*[2] and for all that time we have been fully sexual, and as we shall see in subsequent chapters, we probably handled sexual desire quite creatively for much of that time. We cannot do justice to ourselves as sexual creatures by simply attending to the experience and social constructions of the past few thousand years. To do so grossly distorts the facts!

We are into the territory of historical study and interpretation. Scholars have already posed the critical questions: 'So what is a history of sexuality a history of?' (Weeks 1986: 21); 'If sexuality is constructed, what is the site of the construction?' (Vance 1984: 10). Posing the right questions is crucial to our research. Indeed, it is the prerequisite for the kinds of answers modern institutions can scarcely envisage or entertain.

Aristotelian influence

We are entering a hermeneutical minefield. Let's begin with Aristotle, the reputable genius from which we take so many key concepts that constitute Western civilisation. For Aristotle, men were sexual, women were not. Men were endowed with a capacity to create new life; they were gifted with the seed, and sex was the capacity whereby the man could deposit the seed in the biological receptacle, called the female womb.

The enjoyment and pleasure of sex was intended primarily for the male, not for the female. And it was important to enhance the man's capacity for such pleasure, because the procreation of the species required such instigation. Whether or not the woman enjoyed the experience was of no consequence. Her role was to bring the seed to fruition, and bear life for future generations.

Now if the biological process – set in place through sexual intercourse – is to work according to plan, the predictable outcome will be that of a male child. The males are needed to keep perpetuating the species. And although females are needed to fertilise the seed and bring it to birth, they never received the same attention as the males. The desired outcome was always a male child! Little wonder that female desiring remains problematic even today!

But females are also born! And Aristotle sought to offer explanations for that unfortunate eventuality. He speculated that if there is a damp south wind blowing at the time of sexual intercourse, that may have affected the male seed; it may have weakened its true potential, and consequently, a 'less-than-fully-human-creature' (namely a female) was the result.

From distortion to dogma

This is how Aristotle thought, and people of his day took his word for it! Moreover, his ideas began to dominate the thinking on human sexuality right across the Western world. Incredibly, we find that Thomas Aquinas in the thirteenth century quotes Aristotle verbatim on this notion that a damp south wind could affect the quality of the male seed, thus resulting in female offspring.

Aristotle bequeathed to us a biology of sex in which it is assumed that the capacity for procreation fulfils all the genuine desires that accompany our sexuality. This flawed interpretation was adopted by St Paul, St Augustine, St Thomas Aquinas, and it also features in many of the great Eastern religions. In all cases, sex is demonised, except for the heterosexual arrangement within monogamous marriage, and even there the fear that irrational desire might prevail still haunts popular sexual morality.

> Augustine was very perturbed by the fact that his sexual organ could move by itself with no permission to do so from him.
>
> *Lisa Isherwood (1999)*

The historical backlog – basically that of the past 4,500 years – is very much a male perpetuation, in which females are consigned to total subjugation. In many ways, they were treated no better than sexual slaves, but, more seriously, they had no forum in which they could contribute to the unfolding exploration of what sex is all about. Their voices were silenced, their bodies enslaved, and their deep desires eroded in the quick-lime of patriarchal rationalism.

Quite rightly, therefore, the French post-modernist philosopher Michel Foucault, from whom we inherit a major study on human sexuality, highlights *power* and not *love* as the dominant characteristic of human sexuality (cf. 1977; 1985; 1986).

> I suspect that the real aphrodisiac in the casuistry of sex is not pornographic depiction, but bureaucratic power ... These days, the most dangerous sins don't seem to come from the pursuit of sexual pleasure, but from the pursuit of power.
>
> *Mark D. Jordan (2000)*

We use sex to exert power. Culturally, we do so by ensuring that there are male offspring to continue the male-dominated traditions, and relationally we do so by prioritising the role of the male in intimate (marital) relationships. The marriage bed is often a covert battle-field in which the male seeks to be the winner – and frequently is! Only in the late 1990s when the European court for human rights granted women the right to sue their husbands for rape, did we begin to acknowledge the hidden violence that has characterised marriage for many a long day.

A dramatic shift of emphasis took place in the sixteenth century. Prior to that time, it was the gendering of sexuality that dominated: everything was geared to the good favour of the male. Now, something new and more subtle came into force. In the sixteenth century the *machine* began to emerge as the dominant metaphor for understanding everything in life. Classical science affirmed that the machine was the image in which everything was to be understood, analysed and construed. The impact on sexuality was horrific.

Sexuality was reduced to biology. It was construed to be a biological process that worked in mechanistic fashion. The male and female were endowed with respective pieces of sexual and reproductive equipment. In operating these jointly in the process of sexual intercourse they were activating a process of production. If appropriately activated, like an efficient productive system, a child would ensue nine months later.

Nobody had the honesty to call it *sex as biological reductionism* but that in effect is what it was. The cold, clinical bluntness was hidden behind a number of more benign descriptions, like that adopted by the Catholic Church at the Council of Trent: *sex for procreation*. It sounds positive and respectful but totally endorses the view that there is nothing more to sex except biology.

Not surprisingly, therefore, when the Catholic Church formulated its first ever theology of Christian marriage, it was stated in one brief sentence: the purpose of Christian marriage is *the procreation of the species*, and that continued to be the official teaching of the Catholic Church on marriage until 1962.

This historical excursus is helpful to assess the corrupting impact on human desiring. The gross distortion of human sexuality created an even more malicious derangement for the human capacity for desire. We inherited a double corruption, and as a species we have scarcely begun to address the ensuing anomaly.

6

The Dislocation of Sexual Desire

A confused understanding of sexuality leaves us with a dys-functional understanding of sexual desire.

The British scholar Jeffrey Weeks (1985, 1991) endorses the notion that a *biological imperative* is at work in our understanding of human sexuality, rendering the naturalising and essentialising of sexuality in general, the privileging of heterosexuality as normative and natural, and the demonising of all other forms of sexual expression as deviant and perverse. Weeks, in conjunction with several contemporary analysts, locates this biological orientation in the rise of Darwinian evolution and Freudian psychology in the nineteenth century.

In my opinion, this short-circuits the real historical background, and the consequent oppression which has endured not just for a few hundred, but for some thousands of years. As indicated in the last chapter, the roots of the biological interpretation are apparent in ancient Greek and Roman cultures, but for a more comprehensive understanding of sexuality then and now, we need to embrace older and deeper precedents, dating back to the rise of patriarchy some 10,000 years ago.[3]

Since the middle of the twentieth century, we evidence a growing weariness with the sexuality of biological reductionism. It even impacted a traditionally conservative institution like the Catholic Church which, in 1962, radically changed its theology of marriage. For Catholicism, marriage henceforth would be perceived as having a dual purpose: (a) the love and intimacy of the couple for each other; (b) the procreation of the species. Desire re-entered the landscape, and this time its presence was acknowledged.

Sex and intimate desire

Already in 1951, the contraceptive pill was released for official medical use. This indicated a shift in the understanding of human sexuality, with a growing universal desire to take the focus off child-bearing, and allow sex to be experienced for its own goodness and fulfilment, as a medium of channelling legitimate human desire for love and affection. There seemed to be surfacing a huge cultural reaction to the biological emphasis of the previous four hundred years. Sex was still perceived as being unique to the couple relation-ship in monogamous marriage, although progressively that too became a more tenuous mooring. An unarticulated conviction pre-vailed that sex was intended to be a joyful celebration of intimacy, love and goodness, and the felt need to separate sex from pro-creation became a central issue for the later half of the twentieth century.

Not until the 1980s did we acknowledge the full scale of what was transpiring. Sex came to be identified with human intimacy whether within or outside a marital relationship. The cultural container, namely monogamous marriage, no longer seemed to be able to con-tain the psychosexual energy. Was this raw repression reaping havoc, a new recklessness of the post-modernist age? Or might there be deeper archetypal energies – secret desires long repressed – coming home to roost? These are questions we must bring to what might well be the profoundest discernment facing the human species at the present time.

> Our longing to be in each other's arms is growing stronger than our need to have a target for our hostility. We would like to come together again. But how? How do we, who are veterans of so much combat in the erogenous zones, learn to love in a new way?
> *Sam Keen (1985)*

Human sexuality has suffered from serious cultural displacement. We have traced its origins to classical Greek anthropology, but it dates back further into the rise of patriarchy as the shadow aspect of the Agricultural Revolution. In both cases we encounter an understanding of human sexuality as predominantly that of a biological drive for the procreation of new human life. In this model, sex is primarily for procreation, and all other aspects, lumped together as instincts, are deemed to be dangerous and destructive. Thus the very foundations of sexual desire are condemned as problematic, deviant and not worthy of serious consideration.

Re-enter eroticism

I agree with those who propose that sexuality is largely about desire, and can be construed as the basis for all human desiring. Sexuality is a form of erotic energy belonging to the primal depths not just of human becoming, but arguably of divine becoming also.

> We think of it in purely personal terms, in contrast with many cultures that treat sex as a sacred cosmic force … Lovemaking is a ritual that invites the Goddess of love to be present. The soul requires that we attend to both the temporal and eternal aspects.
>
> *Thomas Moore (1998)*

Consequently, we grossly distort its meaning and seriously jeopardise its impact when we reduce it to a biological process. We dispense with the very elements through which desire can be mediated authentically. And without those elements we are left with a behavioural arrangement which cannot satisfy our deep longings, one that leads to displacement and frustration as our desires veer in the direction of deviant behaviours, compulsive tendencies and often outright addictions.

Only when we embrace a sexual understanding that honours this deeper picture of reality will we see sexuality itself in a more positive light. We will then stand a better chance of understanding the human capacity for desire for what it really is: not merely another genetic endowment, or psychological propensity, but *an erotic quality touching the very core of divinity itself.* I'll return to this exploration in Part Two.

For now, I want to stay with my overview of those forces that corrupt our capacity for desire. With such a dysfunctional sexuality, it will not come as a surprise that desire becomes corroded in other serious ways. Other forces seize the opportunity to placate the raw hunger of unfulfilled desire. Political and economic strategists enter the fray.

7

Our Desire to Be in Control

Much of the irrational fear of desire belongs to our human addiction to power and control.

Amy J. Elias (2001) claims that *post-modernism* is a form of traumatic imagination pulled between two desires:

(a) the political desire to manage and control the physical violence of the twentieth century;
(b) the socio-psychological desire to escape into a more predictable, structured and 'safe' future.

Faced with such an insecure world, we double our efforts to protect ourselves, but ironically we are doing so against the very forces that we ourselves have invented and continue to perpetuate even today.

We desperately desire security and predictability. But desire cannot be reduced to a set of anthropocentric strategies of control, and every attempt to do so inevitably leads to the corruption of desire. As desire becomes progressively undermined, people become frustrated and resort to violence. A vicious cycle is being perpetuated.

A history of reductionism

Reductionism has been around much longer than most scholars are prepared to acknowledge. We assume it has always prevailed within the ambit of the human desire to control reality. We humans seem to have an innate desire to reduce things down to the essentials that we can manage and control. Our research is deemed to be rigorous and objective when we have removed all the extraneous factors, and we believe we have reached an outcome that is pure and real.

> Our world now is literalized. What was once rich in meaning, a subject responsive to many deep and sublime interpretations, becomes nothing more than an object to be analysed, dissected and commodified.
>
> *Sallie McFague (2001)*

But this methodology fails to acknowledge the central role of subconscious forces, and the desires they awaken. The explicit goal of a rigorous outcome is not really about truth but about power. Who will be empowered by this new 'truth' and how effective will it be to validate the right to power, and not the power of truth? Rationality has come to the fore; the masculine values of power and domination take priority.

And we assume it has always been like this! That is a convenient assumption which might well be the greatest delusion modern humans entertain. Reductionism as we know it today is a by-product of prehistoric times when humans first began to take ownership of land in early agricultural times. For almost 10,000 years we humans have devised a system of portioning out reality to the most powerful competitors. It began with the land, and subsequently led to a whole range of institutionalised strategies of management and control. It dominates economics and politics in the modern world.

In classical Greek times we enforced the philosophy of divide-and-conquer by prioritising the rational (male) mind. Aristotle, in *The Nichomachean Ethics*, claims that reason more than anything else constitutes the male soul. This enduring conviction dominates every sphere of contemporary life, eluding the attention of most critics. Val Plumwood is a notable exception: 'dominant forms of reason – economic, political, scientific and ethical/prudential – are failing us because they are subject to a systematic pattern of distortions and illusions in which they are historically embedded and which they are unable to see or reflect upon' (2002: 16).

The rational mindset was reinforced by the rise of classical science in the sixteenth century and by the literalism underpinning much of the Christian religion after the rise of Protestantism with the emphasis on fidelity to God's *word*. Long before the rise of logical positivism in the nineteenth and twentieth centuries, literalised rational discourse enjoyed an unquestioned supremacy. Although now dented by the growing scepticism and cynicism of our time, it still clings to its rigid hegemony.

The cult of minimalism

Once we prioritised the rational method, we progressively undermined and eventually demonised much of the older wisdom that had sustained humans, and their desires, in a very different way. We set humans over the earth and indeed beyond it. We refused to look – and still do – at what life might have been like when humans lived in a more convivial, interdependent relationship with the earth. We dismissed it – and still do – as primitive, barbaric, undifferentiated, pagan, etc. Eventually, we become so self-righteous in our myopic arrogance that we condemn ourselves to a claustrophobic 'civilisation' that causes much spiritual and psychological estrangement in our true nature.[4]

And at this stage one runs the risk of losing the reader. The emerging picture gets too big for minds made small by reductionism. Many of us have been so indoctrinated by the two-thousand-year benchmark that anything bigger than that smacks of a flight into fantasy. And that is a short step from the frequent accusation I receive: I am just a new-age nostalgic, enamoured by a golden age in the past that has no meaning for the present or for the future.

In fact, I don't believe in golden ages! It seems to me that all creation mirrors Tennyson's astute observation that nature is 'red in tooth and claw'. Every age is a 'good enough' age, with its mixture of paradox and promise. My concern is the subverted wisdom that distorts the power of human desire. We, humans, have inhabited the earth for an estimated 6,000,000 years. We share an embodied story within the planet that cannot be evaluated, understood or appreciated within the reductionistic time frames of 2,000 or 10,000 years. My plea is that we honour the human story for what it really is, and not just its fabricated, minimalised narrative of merely a few thousand years.

The fact that we don't have detailed rational or scientific knowledge of our distant past does not justify the crude reductionism whereby we feel justified in dismissing or ignoring over 90 per cent of our existence on earth. Nor can we justify any longer the selective suppression of information that does not meet the contemporary criteria of scientific rationalism, or so-called revealed religious truth. We have archaeological, anthropological, mythological and artistic artefacts that can reveal substantial information to people who can discern with creativity and imagination. Then, we get access to a bigger picture in which human desire begins to look quite different.

Meanwhile, we are left with a broken fragmented view of reality. This fragmentation is a form of violence. We have violated the truth of who we really are and how we function more creatively in the world. Having done violence to ourselves we then project that same violence on to several aspects of creation. We have given birth to a rather violent world, in which our deeper desires stand little chance of being honoured or accommodated.

8

Violence and the Desire for Control

Violence is often associated with desire out of control, but control itself is the problem.

With violence so prevalent in the modern world, it is not surprising that desire is often linked to violence. Specialists of several disciplines consider humans to be innately violent; violence is sometimes traced to bad parenting (Alice Miller), to the fractured relationships which characterise patriarchal society (Carol Gilligan; Robin Morgan), to the evolutionary need for aggression (Lorenz; Colin Morris), to the need to defend property (Ellacuria), as a consequence of State relationships (Weber), and to mimesis and scapegoating (René Girard).[5] Consequently, we behave according to our base nature, unless socially invented mechanisms can help us restrain this unruly desire. Religion, it is claimed, served this purpose in the past, but with religion now so widely discredited, the floodgates of our destructive desiring are wide open, making the twentieth century one of the most violent epochs known to our species.

The aetiology of human violence is based on several questionable assumptions. Some attribute our violent urges to the fact that we are descended from the animals, whom we perceive to be fundamentally aggressive and violent. The social sciences in general adopt the Darwinian view which attributes violence and aggression to the processes of natural selection, in which violence is deemed necessary to weed out the weaker strains. Religions tend to attribute the violence to a fundamental flaw named as Original Sin in the

Christian religions, while several political systems deem the violence of warfare a prerequisite for peace and security.

> We are not going to war "in the name of peace" as deceitful rhetoric so often declares, but rather for war's own sake: to understand the madness of its love.
>
> *James Hillman (2004b)*

A number of these ideas coalesce in one of the leading theories of our time, namely that of mimetic desire elucidated by a French philosopher, René Girard (1977; 1986; also, web page: www.en.wikipedia.org/wiki/Rene_Girard). A brief overview of his theory will indicate the short-sightedness through which many contemporary theorists misconstrue the existence of violence in the human species today.

Desire and rivalry

For Girard, and his disciples, human violence is deemed to be as old as humanity itself. According to Girard, we have always been a violent species; to resolve our violent tendencies we invent scapegoats, and unless we all follow the radical example of the Christian Jesus – who allegedly destroys the power of the scapegoat by assuming it himself – then the cycle of violence will continue unabated.

For Girard, the capacity for desire is the root of the problem. From early infancy, our desires entangle us in covetousness and envy, creating widespread rivalry whereby others desire what we also long for. We begin to compete for the same goods. This inevitably leads to conflictual behaviour, reaching a climax with the identification of a scapegoat whose sacrifice temporarily restores peace. This creates a culture of scapegoating and victimisation which Girard claims has characterised the human species over several thousands of years.

For Girard, the only example in the history of humanity in which the dilemma of violent desire is resolved is in the life and death of Jesus of Nazareth. He interprets the Gospel story as that of an innocent victim who was scapegoated, not by God, but by the collective victimisation of violent humanity. The innocent one bore the sins of violent desiring, and exposes the demonic guilt-transference, repudiating scapegoating, not just once but for all time. By becoming the 'redemptive' scapegoat, Jesus exposes the fallacy and undermines the power of all victimisation.

Girard does not draw parallels with the other great religions, and tends to dismiss ancient myths of sacrifice as ways of circumventing (or avoiding) the encounter with violence and scapegoating which, for him, was achieved most authentically by Jesus of Nazareth.

Questionable assumptions

All Girard's evidence is gleaned from the past 5,000 years. This is impressive to mainline academic scholarship which tends to consider everything before that time as primitive, unreliable and inferior compared with the more advanced, sophisticated culture of the past 2,000 to 3,000 years. Several faulty assumptions come into play here; they need to be reconsidered bearing in mind the following important insights:

- Humans have inhabited planet earth for an estimated six million years. Our ability to survive and thrive throughout that entire time is governed by our capacity for desire. It cannot be adequately explained by evidence gleaned from the past 5,000 years.
- As a human species much of our evolutionary unfolding transpired in a symbiotic relationship with the earth, its seasons, rhythms and energies. Ever since the rise of classical Greek culture, we have condemned that symbiotic relationship with the earth as one of undifferentiated entanglement that kept us ignorant, primitive and unenlightened. That assumption is largely based on a massive projection from the present on to our ancient past. There are other more benign and informed ways of reading our socio-historical past (e.g., Abram 1996), leading to a very different assessment of life and culture in ancient times.

> We rattle around in nihilism, unmet primal needs, assorted addictions … Unlike our hunter-gatherer forebears, we no longer consistently integrate our freedom of movement as animals and our freedom of thought as humans.
> *Bruce Wilshire (1998)*

- Evidence from the Palaeolithic era (40,000–10,000) indicates that our species lived in relative peace and harmony with a highly developed capacity for art, music and sculpture (more in Mithen 2005). During that same time – as for much of the previous several thousand years – we continued to live in close harmony with nature. Desire was channelled much more creatively, indicating that the large-scale violence we witness today was largely unknown.

- About 10,000 years ago, we encounter the Agricultural Revolution, instigating a sudden rise in population, and a new Ice Age in the current European landmass. Humans began to evolve a very different orientation to the land and to life generally. A new aggressive, violent streak begins to surface, activating the strategy of divide and conquer. Modern patriarchy was born; kings evolved for the first time; so did warriors riding on horseback, and the notion of a sky-God was postulated – probably for the first time in human history. From now on Girard's culture of mimetic violence makes a great deal of sense, as does Hillman's analysis of war as an 'archetypal' feature of human culture (Hillman 2004a).

- Girard's interpretation of Christian revelation endorses much of what Christian theology has taught, and Christian praxis has embraced, about the salvific power of Christ's death and resurrection. His ideas reinforce the notion that a certain quality of heroic suffering can change the course of human civilisation for all time. Many Christians embrace this view, but many more question it in the light of the enormous violence that has been exerted in the name of the Christian faith (Ray 1998; Brock and Parker 2007). Whatever may be the theoretical significance of Girard's theory, it is unlikely to enhance Christian faith in a world where more and more people experience Christianity as a religion that carries many vestiges of oppression and violent disregard for people and planet alike.

Violence and frustrated desire

I suggest that a more fruitful line of inquiry should focus on the violence that arises when legitimate desire is consistently thwarted. When people fail to bring their potential to realisation, when every achievement is measured by a price that has to be paid, when legitimate pleasure is persistently being diverted into pain, then frustration arises in the human soul and violent reaction is not an unreasonable outcome.

Peaceful living arises from an inner sense of harmony and fulfilment. Not an outcome of perfection with all the untidy bits eliminated, but a realistic sense of accomplishment in a world where people seek each other's welfare, the fulfilment of mutual desire, rather than victimising each other, in a dispensation of fierce competition. Utopian though it may sound, there is another way of living, more congruent with human welfare, and far more beneficial to the earth we inhabit.

9

Co-opted by Consumerism

*Our capacity for desire has been usurped and perverted by the
lure of modern consumerism.*

Many people today judge their success in life by what they can
purchase and own. And often the more we have the more we crave
for. It is sometimes suggested that our tendency to accumulate many
possessions is an attempt to fill an inner emptiness. We assume this
to be some type of psychological or spiritual deficiency. As I shall
indicate in later chapters, it is a much more complex issue with
cosmological, mystical and psycho-sexual dimensions to it.

Our struggle to satisfy human desire appropriately can easily be
derailed and misguided. With consistent neglect of basic human
needs, e.g., psychosexual and spiritual ones, the tendency to compensate becomes an inescapable survival strategy. This is the
allurement on which so many forces today make coinage. The
human psyche becomes bombarded by promises, so alluring, but on
examination so shallow and fruitless. Commercialisation is among
the leading pundits.

For the purposes of this study, I want to review four aspects of
commercialisation and briefly indicate how they corrupt the human
capacity for desire:

1. *Capitalism.* Several human desires constellate around money and
the role it plays in human life. Capitalism is not merely an economic
system, but more importantly one of ontological significance. Bell
(2001: 3) explains: 'Capitalism extends its reign far more than
merely fostering a particular mode of production and division of
labour; it is best understood as an ensemble of technologies that

disciplines the constitutive human power, desire' (also Deleuze and Guattari 1983).

Capitalism, and its contemporary counterpart globalisation, has subverted a number of key human emotions that nourish and sustain our capacity for desire:

- In many contemporary situations, money has become a god unto itself. Deprived of money, people feel totally disempowered; life seems pointless.
- Earning money has become a form of cultural compulsion which has very successfully undermined the fundamental meaning of work as a mode of creative expression.
- Because the desire to work, as an outlet for creative expression, has been subverted, formal, paid work fails to fulfil our basic spiritual and psychological needs.
- To compensate, capitalism has invented several escape mechanisms, such as shopping, the drug culture and a range of psychotherapeutic services.

> Capitalism alienates the individual from pleasured relationships as a means of producing the unrealizable desire. It exploits the unlimited space of desire by constantly creating more desire ... the dislocated desire of late capitalistic exchange.
>
> *Jeremy R. Carrette (2005)*

2. *Advertising*. Human desiring is mediated through reflection, intuition, imagination and rational thought. These have all been taken over by the indoctrinating culture of capitalism. We are all the victims of a subtle but powerful indoctrination that firstly conquers our capacity for desire and then distorts it so that we desire what the market wants us to purchase. Our capacity to make discerning choices and mature judgements, of a type that would honour our deepest desires, has been seriously undermined.

> Corporate advertising executives long ago became aware that it is highly lucrative to begin conditioning very young children to value individual materialism over family and community. The average child is exposed to more than forty thousand television commercials each year.
>
> *David C. Korten (2006)*

Computer companies frequently donate equipment and software

to educational establishments particularly in socially deprived areas or in impoverished communities in two-thirds world countries. On the surface their generosity is impressive. But every time a child opens the computer, she is bombarded by a slick, colourful advertisement for the computer company itself. And while using the computer, at any moment, a range of other impressive adverts will pop up on screen. Yes, the school can educate in computer technology, but meanwhile the computer company is doing probably a more effective job in subduing the child's capacity for desire, turning him or her into a well-rounded robot-like consumer.

3. *Consumerism*. This is the most widespread addiction of our times. Saving money is an enormous struggle for millions in the contemporary world. We feel we must spend, even for the sake of spending. And the subtle indoctrination of the competitive market compels us to strive and be as good as everybody else in terms of current fashions, designer ware and technological accessories. Shopping is the leading religion in the world today, far more engaging and meaning-producing than any form of religious worship.

> The dominant religion of our time is economism. The God of this religion is endless economic growth; its priests are economists; its evangelists are advertisers; its laity are consumers and its Church is the shopping mall. Virtue is called competition, and vice is inefficiency. Salvation comes through shopping alone.
>
> *John Cobb (1991)*

Consumerism consumes our desires and passions. It drives us to purchase accessories that we really don't need but we can't resist. It creates forms of psychic hunger that require nurturance above the ordinary, and far beyond the culture of sustainable limits. We become overwhelmed by inordinate desire, and can easily become the victims of addictive drives.

4. *Addictions*. Excessive attachment is the corollary to the cult of consumerism. Today we hear of addictions we never heard of before. New variants seem to arise almost annually. One time alcoholism was considered to be the most widespread addiction, but now drugs, gambling and compulsive sexual acting-out belong to the list. Far more destructive to human desiring are our addictions around body-image, fast-foods, designer-fashions, sport and evangelical

religiosity. Moderation has been deleted from the list of culturally desirable virtues. Every desire is hyped-up, exaggerated, stretched to limits that continuously aggravate the spirit and drive the irrational mind.

Our deep desire for ultimacy gives way to a wild hunger (see Wilshire 1998) not easily subjected to a healthy discipline. And our educational systems, themselves subverted by the addictive culture of capitalism, fail dismally to enlighten young or old about what is really going on, never mind give the skills to think more critically. Our educational establishments reinforce the addictive lure by affirming the fierce competition which exposes our entire culture to increasing levels of addictive pain.

The addictive grip of consumerism

In the closing decades of the twentieth century, addictive be-haviours became the subject of much study and research. Beyond the stereotypical focus on alcohol and drugs, gambling and sexual compulsiveness drew much attention. Although some people acknowledge the addictive grip of shopping and wealth accumula-tion, few are prepared to name this new addiction for what it really is. It may well be the greatest threat to desire that we have known as a human species.

Reinforced by slick, captivating advertising, the desire to shop is exacerbated and exaggerated. Much of what we purchase today is not deeply satisfying (see Ritzer 2004). Goods are not intended to last long and, therefore, are quickly discarded to be replaced by the newest fad. Even the food we eat is often superficial and not very nourishing. So, we have to eat more frequently or add supplements to compensate for the poor quality of our diets.

Advertising has effectively indoctrinated young minds, and some not so young, as clothing is judged not by true value, or even aesthetic taste, but by designer label. Fashions come and go at an increasingly rapid rate, depending on how much advertisers can woo and in-doctrinate the gullible public. A new kind of compulsiveness charac-terises our times, leading inevitably to novel forms of addiction and a range of emotional illnesses. Even the need for counselling and therapy has itself become a consumer commodity, often serving as 'a sedative for persons hooked on (or bound to) the capitalist order' (Bell 2001: 98; also Carrette and King 2005: 64ff.).

And nobody is naming the foundational issue at the root of the problem, namely the fact that we are people of desire whose basic humanity can neither survive nor flourish without nourishing our desires. It is not a case of getting rid of desire, nor mitigating it to moral and cultural values, but rather acknowledging and appropriating its deeper meaning. Then, we can begin to discern what is truly fruitful for the nurturance of desire, enabling us to name and confront the many deleterious effects of our consumer and capitalistic culture.

10

Political Structures Frustrate Desire

To fulfil desire, humans have invented social and political institutions that are rapidly outliving their usefulness.

We all assume that the *nation state* is the cultural organism best suited to progress and the good ordering of human affairs. We consider the nation state to be the normative institution through which democratic government can function. And with democracy flourishing, we believe that all needs can be met in a good-enough way, and the desires of the human heart can be honoured!

The nation state

And we have inherited a kind of unspoken patriarchal assumption, as powerful as it is subtle. *The nation state is a divine endowment*: God speaks to 'the nations'; God relates with the earth through the nations. In the Judaeo-Christian tradition God loves creation by selecting one particular nation to be the model for all the others. And God rewards the Jewish nation for its fidelity by fighting on its side and at times brutally subduing its enemies. While Christianity has abandoned a good deal of this violent patriarchal rhetoric, it still carries weight in several of the great religions, most notably in Islam.

Richard Falk (2001: 39) provides an important historical context to these reflections. The concept of the nation state, as we know it today, is a European invention which came to the fore after the

Peace of Westphalia in 1648. Ironically, one of its envisaged functions was to dislodge the monopoly of religion over political activity, while at the same time protecting religious freedom within the context of national governance.

The nation state carries a kind of cultural validation that is virtually impossibly to unmask. It is widely assumed to be the most efficient and effective way to rule and govern and to satisfy the cultural and political aspirations of the masses. These are assumptions virtually unquestioned in the contemporary world. Yet, common sense alone can see through the disparity and superficiality of these claims.

Many nation states are still run as oligarchies. Dictators, claiming absolute power and using the army and police to maintain unquestioned control, operate in several countries. In these situations, people have little say in what affects their lives. Their deepest desires get scant recognition, but for the majority of humans, that's the way things are. And most people see little or no prospect of change.

Western richer nations laud their commitment to democracy and the many 'freedoms' which millions assume go with the democratic mode of governance. But credibility is growing thin, and allegiance is growing weary. Young people in particular see through the façade. The fact that people have the right to vote provides the option to choose a particular government, but what that government does while in power is largely up to their own political strategies and not up to the will of the electorate. And rarely in the West today does a politician come out of politics poorer than when s(he) went in. For most politicians, the so-called *service to the people* renders far more service to the politicians themselves than to those they are called to govern or serve.

> Democracy is in crisis because politics has become empty. The economy takes over as the sole norm, sole absolute value, the sole ultimate reference point ... Never has the economy enjoyed such a radical dictatorship.
>
> *Jose Comblin (1998)*

The State in jeopardy

Governance exercised through political structures is intended to serve the populace in terms of procuring and securing basic needs, and people's daily desires to live creatively and generatively in the world. For millions in our world, this does not happen. The prevailing political systems leave many people bitterly disappointed. Little wonder that disillusionment and cynicism are on the increase.

And these days, frequently, it is not the fault of governments themselves. The institution of the nation state, described by Richard Falk (2001: 7) as 'a profoundly ambiguous political animal', has become a great deal more problematic than most people realise. With the rise of globalisation and trans-national corporations commandeering money, trade and resources, the nation state is no longer in control. In the year 2000 CE, of the one hundred richest organisations on earth fifty-two were trans-national corporations, which means that only forty-eight were nation states. Today, McDonald's has a bigger financial budget than any African country with the exception of South Africa.

Yet, people continue to look to the nation state and to national governments to deliver the wherewithal for happiness and prosperity. But if the governments are not really in control of their own national affairs – and individual states cannot be in control if they have subscribed to World Trade Organisation (WTO) protocol – then how can they deliver on what their people yearn for? In many cases, the nation state is at the mercy of trans-national corporations, whose financial control and trade incursions have been sanctioned by the monopolised power of the WTO. And within that prerogative are the rights for corporations to commandeer local resources, whether it be food-products, minerals, medicines, or even tissue samples of indigenous people; corporations then impose a new blueprint (called a *patent*) whereby nobody else can sell that product except one or other trans-national corporation.

Strictly speaking, it is not savage capitalism that has distorted human desire but rather the validation and reinforcement provided by the nation state. The State lures the citizens into a subtle form of subservience, giving the illusion that people have a real say in what goes on, and giving the false impression that people's real needs matter to those who govern. This two-fold deception has struck deep roots in the contemporary psyche. It will require a major shift of consciousness to alert people to what is really going on. It will take something of a quantum leap in human creativity to dream up alternatives to this corrosive influence we have colluded with for far too long.

11

Colonising Desire on the Global Market

Globalisation colonises human desire with empty, but highly alluring, promises.

Globalisation is a mixed blessing. In our highly connected world, it is inevitable that trade also becomes more global, and millions enjoy the ensuing benefits. And the range of products available on global markets exhibits a cultural diversity unknown to previous generations. In theory we are all the richer for that, but with one piercing enigma: it is those who already have most that have most to gain!

Unfortunately, corporate colonialism disempowers extensively, and in ways that tend to be covert and subtle. Boasting that more people can now enjoy better food, medicine and drinking water – usually at such a high price that the burden of international debt becomes exorbitant – the corporations alienate people from their relationship to the land and its resources, and impose Western norms in ways that are often highly destructive to health, well-being and the richness of local cultures.

The homogenisation of culture

And assuredly there are examples where it seems to work. The body can adjust to eating fast-food, and cultures can adjust to everybody wearing Nike trainers and Adidas tee-shirts. Meanwhile, few realise the damage being done to mind and spirit when cultural homogenisation compels us all to think alike, wear the same clothing, play the same music, and mimic the cultural tyrant whose propaganda has eaten deep into our inner souls, serving false desires while subverting those that are real and genuine.

> When the individual no longer knows by what his soul is sustained, the potential of the unconscious is increased and takes the lead. Desirousness overpowers him, and illusory goals set up in the place of the eternal images excite his greed.
>
> *Carl G. Jung (in Goodchild 2001)*

As highlighted in the penetrating analysis of George Ritzer (2004), globalisation has robbed millions of any realistic hope to meet their legitimate desires in a meaningful way. Even in the Western richer nations the alienation is visible. Farmers struggle to make ends meet and increasingly are subject to a welter of international conditions dictating what they can produce and how they must produce, effectively alienating them from the very land entrusted to their care.

The manufacturing community suffers increasingly from cultural dislocation. They have no idea where raw products come from, and are often totally unaware of the cheap, slave or child labour that may have been involved in producing these products. Nor are they privy to where the products will be sold since that depends on a whole range of trade regulations in which workers often have no say. Little wonder that alienation from work – with billions of dollars wasted every year in work-related sickness – is so rampant. And if we humans are alienated from our work, then several aspects of our life and well-being are under the threat of estrangement.

The ideology of globalisation

The political and economic strategies of globalisation reap immediate benefits for those who are already advantaged. Even for the well-off long-term prospects are at best unsure. Globalisation is preoccupied with one desire above all others, namely the desire to make money. Consequently, the core strategy has a kind of heartlessness built into it, a kind of ruthlessness that has little real concern either for people or the planet they inhabit. In the name of one grossly over-riding desire, it railroads all other desires, particularly those most essential to long-term human meaning.

Market is conceived as the sole arbitrator of the future of the peoples. Neo-globalism is thoroughly an all encompassing anti-state ideology ... The very concept of citizenship has become a beleaguered idea at the advent of globalisation.

Anthony Kalliath (in Kadankavil 1999)

Can the process be halted? Can it be reversed? If humanity has any hope of living meaningfully on the planet, then this crude imperialistic strategy needs to be challenged. Some think, perhaps, hope, that the whole thing is so alien to human and planetary well-being that it will eventually implode and collapse in on itself. Perhaps that was what was happening to the WTO at Cancun in 2003 and, a few months later, to the FTAA (The Free Trade of the Americas) in Miami. These were irruptions by two-thirds world countries who could no longer tolerate the gross negligence of fundamental desires, and, despite their sworn allegiance to WTO and FTAA, some decided to pull the plug. They could no longer ride on the juggernaut of globalisation, and they took the risk in opting out.

The protests at WTO meetings over the previous decade began to bear fruit. Alternative NGOs and several other ground movements expressed anger and frustration at the gross manipulation of the corporations and the serious undermining of authentic human desire. New networks took up the cause, such as the International Forum on Globalisation (www.IFG.org). Ground action and creative thinking built up a new alternative consciousness and it bore fruit at Cancun and Miami. Now the energy needs to be re-directed towards alternatives based on *localisation* (Hines 2000) rather than the impersonal bureaucratic mega-machine of globalisation.

Meanwhile, the USA continues to perpetuate the philosophy of divide and conquer, seeking to woo individual countries into the delusory net of satisfying superficial desires through financial deals that look lucrative and attractive but are extremely damaging to local resources and to long-term sustainability. A great deal of education is still needed to stem the tide of consumerist allurement.

A new political landscape?

In our globalised world today, meeting needs through civil society is a very different type of engagement from that of a few decades ago. Governments try to convince the citizenry that things are pretty much as they always were, and that individual governments rule quite effectively through the mechanism of the nation state. This is a blatant lie, a gross deception, an attempt to pull the wool over people's eyes.

> Increasingly, we see the denouement of the nation-State as a viable unit of governance; becoming too big for the small problems of its own local populations and at the same time too small for the big problems of global relations and ecosystems.
>
> *Hazel Henderson (1988)*

The nation state is largely an anomaly in our time. It maintains a veneer of cultural distinction, uniqueness and focused control. But in practice, no state can go it alone anymore and, in terms of financial independence, the real power is in trans-national commerce and not in the coffers of indigenous governments.

All the while, the earth itself becomes more and more of an object to be used and exploited. The more it happens the more humans become disenchanted and alienated from the very organism which begets life and meaning. On that slippery slope humanity is on a downward slide of frightening proportion. Many theorists believe it is already too late; the destructive trends are irreversible. Maintaining hope and optimism is often an up-hill struggle.

The pain of disconnection

More than anything else our disconnection from the earth is probably the severest form of pain we know today. The problem is that most people don't feel it consciously. We have invented a vast array of sedatives, drugs, alcohol, hedonism, workaholism, religiosity and pseudo-therapies to rationalise our alienation. The psychologist Otto Rank recognised the problem some years ago when he wrote: 'When religion lost the cosmos, society became neurotic. And we needed to invent psychology to deal with the neurosis' (quoted in Fox 1984: 66). It was not just religion that lost the cosmos, it was primarily the patriarchal rule of order.

In a sense therefore, globalisation can be viewed as cosmic justice coming back to haunt humanity. Globalisation is humanity's confused attempt to become a global species once more. The vision is right, but the strategy is wrong, specifically because it is too narrowly focused on money, power and exploitation of the earth as a commodity. For humans, the earth is not intended to be a commodity, and that is where the alienation becomes most pernicious.

Reconnecting with the earth – with the whole earth – is the single greatest challenge now facing us as a human species. Nothing short of such a new planetary amalgamation will guarantee the meeting of our deepest needs and the realisation of our true desires. Then we can re-learn what it means to be human. Then we can begin to come home to where we truly belong.

12

Desire and the Lack of Meaningful Work

Meaningful work channels desire, but current work practices fail dismally in this regard.

About two hundred years ago, humans worked for the sheer joy of doing so. As a result of our work there was produce from the land or from the workshop that was exchanged according to human need. I needed some extra clothing and you needed wheat to make flour to bake your own bread. We exchanged wheat for clothing.

Today we call it the *gift economy*. We gifted each other with the wherewithal we needed to live meaningfully on the earth. And many were much closer to the earth, tilling and cultivating it for the joy and satisfaction of doing so. Work was not equated with money. The idea of linking a financial earning to a piece of work had not yet evolved. Industrialisation introduced this new way of accessing wealth. It certainly was more efficient and improved the quality of life for millions. But we paid a big price for this culture of moniterised enterprise.

Feeling useful

Sigmund Freud made the astute observation that humans have two foundational needs: the need to love and the need to *work*. Psychologically, we devote great attention to the former but scant attention to the latter. That the one may be as important as the other may come as something of a surprise. We struggle to get many things right in terms of those friendships and relationships through which we mediate love, but work is something we largely take for granted. And because we identify work with money, we fail to attend to the spiritual and psychological significance of work in our lives.

> Desire shatters the economy of things; it disputes the tyranny of objects.
>
> *Wendy Farley (2005)*

Work provides the environment for the creative release, articulation and fulfilment of our basic need to feel valued and useful. At a more subtle and subconscious level, work is the medium through which we contribute to making the world a better place. It enables and empowers us to feel more at home in the world, to belong interdependently and to contribute constructively. Through our work we grow into becoming co-creators with those other evolutionary forces that shape the universe.

Rightly, therefore, Matthew Fox (1994) describes work as a form of ritual. Ritual is often confused with religious rite and ceremony. Ritual predates formal religions by thousands of years. We humans had adopted ritual behaviours long before formal religion ever evolved, and several rituals employed by our ancient ancestors relate to the seasons, the use of land, cycles of fertility, etc. 'Ritual heals and celebrates,' writes Fox (1994: 298), 'and brings the microcosm into relationship with the macrocosm, joining the work of our daily lives and the Great Work of the universe.'

In this context work is not just about activism, a set of physical or mental activities to achieve a task and earn a reward. Ideally all work should be playful and joyful, generative and celebratory, a far cry from the drudgery that characterises so much work today. Before work became identified with earning money, people worked for the sheer joy of doing it, and that joy arises from an innate sense of creativity and accomplishment that accompanies fulfilling work.

Work as birthing

These positive characteristics also apply to difficult work. Whether it is work that is physically or mentally demanding, emotionally draining as in the care of the sick and elderly, or spiritually exerting in times of anguish and trauma, work that arises from the inner desire to live creatively will always feel energising no matter how demanding it may be. Here we touch on the paradox of birth-giving. For a mother, pregnancy, labour and delivery can be painful, and, despite modern medical advances, child-bearing still carries health risks for many women. But the joy that accompanies the birth of new life, the sense of accomplishment and the unspeakable sense of co-creating in this unique way, all contribute to integrating the accompanying pain and suffering.

This ability to combine pain and joy, to hold the paradox written into every aspect of creation, is rarely realised in our working lives. The joy is rarely achieved, and the pain is seldom talked about. In other words, we drift along with a system over which we have little real influence. We judge its value, not in terms of personal satisfaction, and less in terms of what it might contribute to the well-being of creation, but in terms of how much wealth or status it will achieve for us. Little wonder that we are so estranged from the deeper meaning of our work! More tragic still is the emptiness we feel inside as some of our deepest desires are so poorly accommodated.

The living wage

Today, we find it hard to envisage work without money. Despite the fact that millions in the two-thirds world are not waged earners, and some of the most nurturing and caring work in the developed nations is not remunerated, we are indoctrinated with the idea that you work for money. And while millions do work for money, in the West at least, it costs millions to keep people in work. Boredom and sickness mean that workers on a large scale under-perform. And many work in jobs that are not congruent with their innate giftedness.

Fundamentally, the desire to work arises out of a human need to be creative. That is how we are 'designed' for life. Deprived of that capacity for meaningful work, we tend to atrophy and become apathetic. Not surprisingly, deviant behaviours set in, and our over-all state of being, physically and emotionally, often reveals the signs of strain. A deep human need is not being met, namely work that will liberate our creative potentials. The consequences can be horrendous.

In time, nature seems to sort out some of its own cultural distortions and, today, we can see a new work ethic in the making. Not, however, until the old model proves sufficiently unwieldy will we let go and opt for creative alternatives. The signs of disintegration are fairly obvious for those who have eyes to see. A culture of formal employment tends to undermine the dignity and giftedness of those who cannot participate, which is in the region of 50 per cent of the population of any Western nation at any one time. Many of those in formal employment do not enjoy their work, cannot bring their best selves into it, and substantial numbers are consistently out of work on sick-leave.

But most dysfunctional of all is the financial cost to countries themselves. To run the present system of paid employment requires a cumbersome, top-heavy bureaucracy; for each individual nation it incurs a heavy financial burden. To rectify this problem, governments are exploring ways of diminishing or regulating pension-schemes. Many people entering the work world in the opening years of the twenty-first century face the prospect of never obtaining a State-granted pension.

But perhaps, more disturbing still, many face the prospect of never obtaining a weekly or monthly wage as *contract labour* rapidly becomes the norm of the future. In this scheme people are paid by the hour, with none of the incentives accompanying the traditional wage. And employment will only be guaranteed for the duration of a specific piece of work, which might be a few years, but in the majority of occasions will be a few months or perhaps a matter of weeks at any one time.

Towards a new work ethic

A paradigm shift will occur whenever the necessities of life are beyond the reach of most citizens. We must critique our professions and suggest ways out of their impasses. The professions themselves exemplify failed relationships in many cases.

Matthew Fox (1994)

The notion of a job for life, with accompanying insurance protection and pensions, fulfilled the human desire for security and for a sense of achievement in life. In many cases, however, it left unfulfilled the desire to feel useful, and the ability to contribute constructively to the evolution of life on planet earth. Work often felt like drudgery and, as indicated above, provided minimal opportunity for the development of people's gifts and talents.

For some years now, social activists and economists exploring alternative models have been proposing new approaches to work. Among these, perhaps the most imaginative and revolutionary is the notion of separating work from the living wage, requiring the nation state to pay a basic wage to every citizen over the age of eighteen years of age. This notion sounds so idealistic and far-fetched that many people dismiss it before considering its radical ramifications. Contrary to popular expectation, research conclusively shows that this strategy would save Western nations millions of dollars annually. Bureaucratically, it is a relatively simple process to administer, and therefore enables a government to reduce significantly the top-heavy administrative machinery needed for the current system.

In greater detail the scheme goes like this:

- Every citizen over the age of eighteen is paid a basic wage that guarantees a good quality of life in terms of access to basic needs, education, health care, etc.
- Those in formal employment pay taxes to the tune of at least 60 per cent, but they also obtain the basic wage.
- Voluntary work, rather than paid employment, becomes the norm, as all citizens are challenged – primarily through a revamped educational system – to contribute to the welfare of life environmentally, culturally and personally.
- Class distinctions would break down. Poverty would be eliminated in time. Unemployment, and its terrible stigma, would cease. People would learn to take pride in their achievements and would be happier in themselves. A much more harmonious culture would ensue, where needs and desires are met in a more responsible way.[6]

Would the system work? Researchers acknowledge that it would require an enormous amount of good will and would require huge numbers to transcend the greed and acquisitiveness that drives the current system. That, in turn, would depend on the quality and quantity of education to make the perceptual and attitudinal shift without which the change is unlikely to happen.

It is all too easy to mount criticism of this visionary resolution, and all too easy to dismiss it in a sinister and cynical way. *But evolution itself may resolve the dilemma for us.* As the job-for-life model, work related to wage-earning, breaks down, we will be forced to look at alternatives, and patching up the existing system is unlikely to provide creative resolutions. This is a paradigm shift with all the trauma and utopia that such transitions bring. The new reality will be different from the old, so new in fact as to be virtually unrecognisable. Exactly what the philosopher Whitehead had in mind when he warned us that it is the business of the future to be dangerous and that major advances in civilisation all but wreck the societies in which they occur.

13

Desire and Forsaken Memory

The patriarchal culture of the past 10,000 years has seriously undermined our capacity for desire which we honoured for most of our previous existence.

Scholars of ancient wisdom work with the assumption that our pre-historic peoples were so enmeshed in nature that they were incapable of developing those more advanced capacities that constitute authentic human well-being. In our undifferentiated state, it is widely assumed, our lives were governed by instinct and impulse; we were closer to the animal than to the human. Many scholars consider the development of language, about 100,000 years ago, to be the first serious cleavage from our primitive origins into the realm of what could be considered true humanity. With the emergence of language we began to think for ourselves and develop capacities for rational thought, abstraction and the use of the imagination.

Projections abound in this type of analysis. Sometimes the behaviours of currently extant tribal groups are cited as collaborative evidence. Occasionally, the data is selectively chosen and misinterpreted out of context. But most serious of all is the cultural and scholarly arrogance whereby we set ourselves up as superior to peoples of other times whom we deem to be primitive, barbaric and basically inhuman.

The lived context

These judgements are often made within the academic realms of the science laboratory, the religious institution, or the educational establishment. Little or no effort is made to understand earlier times and cultures in situ. For long, we assumed that humans are prone to violence, because animals behave violently – on the evidence that animals behave aggressively when observed in laboratory conditions. But scholars such as Jane Goodall (2001) and Frans de Waal (1997; 2005) have amply demonstrated that animals in the wild, in their natural habitat, behave very differently, and in most cases tend to be far less violent and aggressive than hitherto assumed. Similarly with humans, because scholars judge extant tribal peoples to behave in primitive fashion – then it is assumed we all did once upon a time. We begin to see through a mode of reasoning that is deeply and dangerously flawed.

What such research fails to highlight are qualities like the befriending of nature and the close connection with land which indigenous peoples often achieve in a uniquely sustainable and spiritually informed way. Here we may well have a pointer to earlier times when our ancestors lived out of a much more convivial relationship with cosmic and planetary life. Interdependence was the key feature and through it humanity thrived. McFague (1997: 60) quotes the Chinese American geographer Yi-Fu Tuan:

> The cosmos of pre-modern man was multi-storied; nature was rich in symbols, its objects could be read at many levels and evoke an emotion-laden response. Science, by contrast, strives to reduce the possibility of multiple readings. A traditional world has the ambiguity and richness of ordinary and ritual speech. The modern world, on the other hand, aspires to be transparent and literal.

What nature desires

To counter this view, religionists tend to invoke one or another argument about a 'fundamental flaw', while others cling to the notion of an innate potential for violence and destruction, all too apparent throughout the twentieth century. I am not arguing for a species that could transcend the limitations of the human condition we know today. I simply want to highlight the fact that when we remain close to nature: (a) we behave differently; (b) we behave in a manner that tends to be more congruent with the unfolding process of creation itself and, as a consequence, (c) the cumulative impact of our behaviour is less violent and less destructive, and

(d) basic human needs tend to be met in a wholesome and healthy way.

> It is no surprise that alienation is one of the chronic diseases of our time, since we have all but lost the sense of connectedness to self, the divine, and nature, all vital components to our fundamental reality.
>
> *Judy Cannato (2006)*

In short, our present relationship with the planet and with the cosmos is largely that of minimalistic functionaries, devoid of intimacy, freedom and creativity. Our deepest desires are neither acknowledged nor mediated appropriately. There is growing evidence to suggest that for our ancient ancestors human needs were met far more creatively than we are achieving today. I am not suggesting we regress; evolution never regresses. I am proposing we can learn from the past, a cumulative wisdom that can enhance and augment our forward movement.

But we are unlikely to choose that option until we break through and dismantle the reductionism within which we are trapped. It has infiltrated every sphere of our existence. Jason Hill (2000) describes it as a form of tribalism constituted largely by our racism, ethnicity and allegiance to the ideology of the nation state. Sallie McFague (1997: 67ff.) attributes this set of perceptions to what she calls 'the arrogant eye' through which we perceive and analyse nature as an object – in a dualistic and disembodied way. Consistently, we miss the larger context. Our dissected, fragmented view of reality always leaves us feeling empty and incomplete.

We are people with a memory, embodied in myths and narratives that we embrace in our story-telling. But our memory has been deranged and our story has been dismembered. Our deep connections with creation's story have been fragmented and desecrated. Retrieving those lost elements and reclaiming their rightful place is the subject material for the remainder of this book.

The Enormous Damage We Have Done to Desire

In Part One, I have reviewed the forces that undermine desire, that reduce it down to a set of human feelings that can be co-opted by the seduction of the market, demonised in the name of religion, sublimated into violent victimisation, or subverted to serve the culture of rational discourse. In all cases, control seems to be the culprit through which we continually miss the goal of our yearnings. Even the philosophers' attempt at a phenomenology of desire has fallen prey to corrupting influences.

Our desire to control desire often falls foul of two extremes: we try to spiritualise it out of existence (as in religion) or we are overwhelmed by its hedonistic lure (as in sex and consumerism). The more we violate the human capacity for desire, the more violent our desiring becomes. The more we try to evade or suppress desire, the more it rebounds to haunt us. Clearly, we are not handling it well, nor are we likely to do so till we understand more holistically what desire actually entails.

Phenomenologists tend to view desire as a capacity of the human brain. It belongs to humans only, and affects behaviour through brain functions predominantly. This analysis suits the current academic climate wherein brain-research (and genetics) is the flavour of the month. But this is an extremely limited viewpoint, incapable of engaging our longings and yearnings in an authentic and meaningful way.

Redeeming desire is an onerous task. A lot of baggage needs to be sorted and disposed of. A lot of misconstrued notions and ideas need to be abandoned. And a great deal of homecoming needs to be embraced. Desiring belongs to who we are innately; it is the erotic awakening that empowers our being and becoming at every stage of our existence. We need to reclaim and reintegrate that which is endemic not just to our well-being, but to our potential for a rich and meaningful life.

Strange though it may sound, we can only retrieve desire when we choose to dehumanise it – more accurately, re-humanise it! We over-identify desiring with the human, largely forgetting that this is a capacity humans have inherited from creation at large. Only when we understand the process on the larger universal scale do we stand a real chance of reclaiming desire in its deeper meaning. That is our challenge for Part Two of this book.

PART TWO

The Rehabilitation of Desire

Eros, archetypal of the lost individual of an addictive society, the individual with a crisis of misplaced desire, will find no way back to psychic integration, and the realisation of his own heart's desire, without an entire cultural revolution.

Mary C. Grey (2003)

14

Desire and the Cosmogonic Eros

Our human capacity for desiring belongs primordially to the cosmic creation itself.

At the heart of all desiring is a yearning for beauty. 'The human soul is hungry for beauty,' writes John O'Donohue (2003: 12, 17). 'We seek it everywhere – in landscape, music, art, clothes, furniture, gardening, companionship, love, religion and in ourselves. No one would desire not to be beautiful. When we experience the Beautiful, there is a sense of homecoming ... The time is now ripe for beauty to surprise and liberate us.'

Our educational and spiritual conditioning suggests that we can only reclaim beauty by mastery and control. Very rightly, John O'Donohue reminds us that *surrender* rather than *mastery* is how we will make the journey to true wholeness. Beauty is mystically suspended between the act of awakening and the act of surrender. Among the awakenings of our time is the growing realisation that we live far from where beauty first originates for us, namely in the earth itself (O'Donohue 2003: 42ff.). The religions inform us that God is the source of this beauty and, therefore, the creator of everything that exists. But, as we saw in Part One, religion itself has not been very successful in honouring its own deep insights.

Beauty, desire and eros

We desire to live beautifully because that is what creation has modelled for us for billions of years. But being creatures who have so alienated ourselves from creation, with its foundational propensity for beauty, desire in our time has lost much of its beauty and its retrieval may well be the single greatest challenge facing humanity today.

Desire – all desire – belongs first and foremost to the cosmic realm of creation. It is the driving force within the intentionality that guides evolutionary becoming. In the words of Wayne Dyer (2004: 4), 'intention is not something you do, but rather a force that exists in the universe as an invisible field of energy.' That which brought forth creative energy in the original flaring forth of the Big Bang, and sustained its emergence over several billions of years, is itself intention or desire (eros). We can describe it as the power that energises energy itself, infusing it with what some evolutionary scholars call 'a preferred sense of direction', persuasively illustrated by John Stewart (2000) as an unrelenting capacity for co-operation in which 'Evolution itself evolves, and living processes get smarter at evolving' (p. 12).

This foundational energy I call *eros*, the fiery fierce, yet subtly gentle, force that brings everything in creation into being. Veronica Goodchild (2001: xxiii) discerns that the God, Eros, lurks in the compelling desire of matter and spirit for each other to recover a lost wholeness. It abides in the depths of creative silence, ever manifesting as that which persuades being to transcend the polar force of non-being, what Swimme and Berry (1992) describe as the paradox of creation and destruction. On this paradoxical evolutionary movement hangs all hope and possibility from the deep ancient past to the present moment.

These two words – *beauty* and *eros* – serve as hinges for the reflections that follow. Our desires are fuelled by the erotic urge through which everything comes into being, from the cosmic galactic structures to the tiny bacteria, invisible to the human gaze. And the desiring heart is sustained and nourished by the beauty that radiates in creation's elegant unfolding. As we shall see, this is not always pleasant to our senses, but for those who can intuit the deeper meaning, there is beauty even in the chaos. Fractal mathematics illustrates this quite graphically (on fractals, see www.wikipedia.org/wiki/Fractal and www.mathsnet.net).

The erotic birthing forth

In my attempt to rehabilitate desire, I want to establish the *cosmic* and *planetary* dimensions and use this foundational understanding throughout the rest of the book. I first encountered this approach in the work of Joel Kovel (1991: esp. Chapter Four, 'Spirit and Desire'), in Hans Jonas's notion of the *cosmogonic eros* (1996; also Haught 2000) and, most recently, in Judy Cannato's inspiring book, *Radical Amazement* (2006). In this context, *eros* exhibits a threefold expression:

(a) *Birthing the new.* Creation never ceases to birth forth new possibilities. A prodigious fertility infuses everything in the cosmic realm. Religions claim that God created the world, but underestimate the world's own capacity for pregnant unfolding.

> The Spirit is the great creative matrix who grounds and sustains the cosmos and attracts it towards the future. Throughout the vast sweep of cosmic and biological evolution she embraces the material root of existence and its endless new potential, empowering the cosmic process from within. The universe in turn is self-organizing and self-transcending ... The Spirit's action does not supplant that of creatures but works cooperatively in and through created action, random, ordered or free.
>
> *Elizabeth Johnson (1992)*

When we postulate a 'fathering' God we inevitably end up with a co-dependent creation. Patriarchal hierarchies are then invoked, and the erotic fertility and creative freedom are subverted. As Ruth Page (1996: 54) demonstrates so well, this approach jettisons both our understanding of God's birthing potential as well as God's role in the process of creation.

(b) *Empowered for connection.* Erotic energy is free but not random. It moves in the direction of relationality. It seeks to connect and in the connections begets new possibilities. We evidence this in the subatomic world of quarks and leptons. They make no sense in isolation. In laboratory conditions they always manifest in twos or threes. Patterns of three also predominate in the galactic and planetary spheres. At the bacterial stage we observe similar connectedness in what Lynn Margulis (1998) calls the process of symbiogenesis. Eros is desire for union, for connection, for relationship.

> We live in a relational world that institutions have considerably impoverished. Society and the institutions which frame it have

limited the possibility of relationships, because a rich relational world would be very complex to manage.

Michel Foucault (1978)

(c) *Its favoured orientation is towards the future*, not towards the past. While organic evolution seems to build on repeated patterns from the past, it is the lure from the future that directs evolutionary becoming. John Haught (2000; 2003) postulates this lure of the future on the basis that God operates out of *promise*, a promise that will always be fulfilled.

> The future, not the dead past, is the foundation upon which the world leans ... Hidden beyond our grasp, in the depths of the future that forever faithfully takes us and our world into itself, there resides the really real ... Theology has conceived of God too much in terms of the notion of a Prime Mover impelling things from the past. Evolution demands that we think of God as drawing the world from up ahead, attracting it forward into the future.
>
> *John F. Haught (2003)*

My preferred interpretation would be to endorse Meister Eckhart's birthing metaphor: 'What does God do all day long: God lies on a maternity bed all day long' (quoted by Fox 2000: 41). Divine creativity forever manifests in birthing new life because the future is worthy of such investment. The future draws forth that which will make the future worthwhile. Evolution does this all the time.

The erotic spirit

Creation is endowed with erotic intentionality. Forever, it seeks and yearns for new expression, for new communion with all that already exists. The driving force behind this powerful yearning is what Christian theology calls the *Holy Spirit*.[7] The inspiring life-force of the divine has imbued and endowed creation from the earliest moments of creation (if there ever was such a point in time), but more significantly the Spirit is the luring attraction of the open-ended future. As Elizabeth Johnson (quoted in Edwards 2004: 47) says, 'The Spirit is the great, creative Matrix who grounds and sustains the cosmos and attracts it towards the future', or in the poetic words of Mark Wallace (2005: 125), 'The Spirit ensouls the earth as its life-giving breath, and the earth embodies the Spirit's mysterious interanimation of the whole creation.'

The erotic lure, therefore, has a twofold orientation. It co-creates and forges deeper communion. It endows evolution's trajectory not merely with a potential for birthing forth ever-new possibility, but also for directing all emergence towards new connectedness. This is the basic orientation towards *co-operation* identified by John Stewart (2000) as the arrow of evolution and by the microbiologist Lynn Margulis (1998) in her theory of symbiogenesis.

How these insights relate with the Darwinian approach is a topic I have explored elsewhere (O'Murchu 2002: 66ff.). My primary concern in the present work is to honour the primordial wisdom upon which creation thrives. Both contemporary science and spirituality suggest that ours is not a random creation, nor is it predetermined (designed) according to some lofty divine master-plan. Rather it is endowed with an inspired erotic wisdom forever desiring the greater life we all yearn for. From this foundational source springs all desire, human and non-human alike.

And without embracing this cosmic dimension we cannot hope to heal the damage we have done to the desiring universe, nor can we, as persons, hope to rehabilitate in a wholesome way that which we have suppressed and ignored for so long.

15

Integrating Desire with the Quantum World View

Desire is a propensity that transcends and defies all attempts at rational explanation.

> Sometimes everything has to be enscribed across the heavens so you can find the one line already written inside you.
>
> *David Whyte (2001)*

Before we can hope to rehabilitate desire, we need to attend to the world-context within which our desires awaken – where they initially seek expression and fulfilment. The older mechanistic view of creation, undergirding a great deal of modern technology, can only entertain desire as an appetite we satiate with material goods and human power. Such a world view is grossly inadequate for the rehabilitation I am exploring in this book.

For much of the patriarchal era of the past 10,000 years, humans regarded the earth as an object for their own use and benefit. The secular materialism of the nineteenth century is the icing on the cake for an anthropocentric domination that is several millennia old. It began to disintegrate in the 1920s when scientists themselves were pushed out of the neat conceptualised world of classical science. New wisdom was unfolding and the old parameters could not hold any longer. A new world view was being born.

In fact, it was quite an old understanding, the one humans had known for thousands of years before the age of patriarchy, one familiar to many of the great mystics. It came to be known as

Quantum Theory, postulating that reality unfolds not in rational, linear segments but in bursts of possibility that defy rational observation or quantification. It was a new way of seeing, that could honour another way of desiring. More importantly, it allowed a new metaphysical question to arise: What does creation itself desire in its unfolding orientation? Echoes of this question can be detected in this résumé statement of Deepak Chopra (2000: 39):

> Creation manifests
> Energy exists.
> Time begins
> Space expands from its source.
> Events are uncertain.
> Waves and particles alternate with one another.
> Only probabilities can be measured.
> Cause and effect are fluid.
> Birth and death occur at the speed of light.
> Information is embedded in energy.

Beyond human control

In this new vision there is no power over, only power with. Playing the power-games of patriarchal domination is deeply alien to the nature of life as exemplified in the quantum vision. Our insatiable desire for control makes no sense in a universe where everything exercises its own sense of control precisely because everything is out of our control.

The goal of our desiring, contrary to popular perception, is not *control* but *surrender*, not human mastery but trust. When we rehabilitate creation's capacity for desire, then human desire stands a much better chance of growth and flourishing. We live in a self-organising universe, where we humans need to have the humility and   wisdom to submit our plans to the greater wisdom of the cosmic and planetary systems. In this understanding the rules of the game go something like this:

• The neat, fixed, unchanging face of reality yields pride of place to fluid flows and quantum fluctuations of creative energy, driven by forces which we humans, at this stage of our evolution, do not even understand, never mind control.

- We transcend the world of rational deductive reasoning – cause and effect don't work any more as we thought they did, and still think they should.
- We encounter a world where every whole is greater than the sum of its parts, and individual parts make little or no sense in their lonely isolation.
- Creation is structured not merely in terms of physical objects, but according to spheres of influence called *fields*, something akin to archetypes in Jungian psychology (see Conforti 1999).
- We are called to befriend a relationally oriented creation in which the capacity to relate is an indelible feature.
- We engage with the particle-wave duality as co-creative participators, always modifying what we engage with, to a greater or lesser degree.
- We inhabit a cosmos of non-locality (Nadeau and Kafatos 1999), in which effects happen at speeds greater than the speed of light and according to dynamics in which the flapping of a butterfly's wing at one end of planet earth can affect the course of a tornado at the other end.
- We encounter a wisdom greater than our own, a consciousness that belongs primarily to cosmic creation and laterally to the human brain (further explored in O'Murchu 2002: 169–81).

Adjusting desires ...

No serious scientist will question the reality of quantum physics, verified in the vast range of practical applications in technology and nano-science. Yet, the scientific community seems to be compulsively committed to subjecting the quantum world view to that of classical science. As a species we seem to find it enormously difficult to embrace a more fluid and open sense of reality. We cannot fully control it, yet we stubbornly pursue an irrational desire for power and domination.

This is the contemporary irrationality that consistently undermines the human capacity for desire and persistently creates human angst and meaningless suffering. The quantum vision articulates a radical orientation of creation without which desiring cannot be honoured. What many consider to be an alternative world view, I want to reclaim as *an authentic world view*. Only when we take this new view seriously do we stand any realistic chance of honouring the desires of the heart. Then, we will desire what creation desires, and true progress stands a better chance of materialising.

Reclaiming this view of reality, and adopting it in daily life, is a formidable responsibility. It is frayed with potential sacrifice and misunderstanding. It involves going against the grain of society's most cherished values and institutions. It is likely to involve huge sacrifices in terms of wealth, status, reputation, and even survival.

We can draw some hope from the fact that people have travelled down this road in previous times, especially mystics and prophets, and dotted around the planet are a few million brave souls who aspire to this ideal. Internet networking is one strategy to keep a sense of connection and mutual support. But, perhaps, the strongest motivation for espousing this ideal, is the growing realisation that time is running out for Homo sapiens in terms of our conventional Western lifestyle. Our desiring is in conflict with that of creation's innate wisdom. When we learn to desire what creation desires, then a new conviviality is possible and both humans and creation can grow and prosper in a new way.

16

Honouring the Cosmic Desire to Belong

Belonging, rather than separation or isolation, provides the global context through which desire is best expressed.

According to Swimme and Berry (1992), everything in creation is characterised by *differentiation*, *autopoiesis* (interiority) and *communion*. These may be compared to three patterns along which creative energy flows. *Differentiation* refers to the absolute uniqueness of everything in creation, rather poetically encapsulated in the phrase: 'every hair on your head is numbered'. *Autopoiesis* describes the self-regulating propensity which features extensively in creation, an innate intelligence similar to the immune system in the human body. *Communion* describes the foundational direction of evolution. Not merely are humans programmed for relationship but so is everything in creation. More accurately, humans relate because creation relates!

The matrix of belonging

These three features, however, cannot be viewed in isolation. They, too, belong to a relational web. They work interactively and co-operatively. The most enduring is the communion, not the differentiation. What unites us determines what each of us becomes and it is in our becoming (flourishing) that connection rather than difference determines our identity. And the flourishing is not a random, meaningless process. It is imbued with meaning and a sense of direction precisely because of the autopoiesis, that deep inner wisdom that animates every stage of the evolutionary process in cosmos, planet and person alike. Theologians like Denis Edwards (2004) and Mark Wallace (2005) would describe it as the inspiring, infusing power of *the Holy Spirit.*

The three movements constitute what modern scientists call quantum fluctuations, incorporating the wave-particle dance that never ceases. One can never determine which aspect is being invoked at any one time, nor who or what is doing the invoking. In a universe of non-local connectedness (cf. Nadeau and Kafatos 1999; www.en.wikipedia.org/wiki/Principle_of_locality), my insecurity might be triggered off by humans slaying an elephant in Southern Africa, just as my joy may be adumbrated by a new flower that has evolved in Australia. Each one of us is a nodal point in a chain of events embracing a complex, intriguing universe.

For many readers these ideas seem far-fetched and idiosyncratic; for religious readers they are likely to evoke fear that the dignity of the human person (and of God) is under threat; for the rationally minded who hold most of the power in our major institutions, they are likely not even to entertain these ideas, never mind try to make sense of them.

The quantum pattern

I deliberately float the quantum context because herein is embedded the deeper layers of human desiring, and herein are the guidelines for the work of rehabilitation I am exploring in these pages. According to quantum physics, our universe:

- is a holon, always needing a greater whole to realise its fuller potential;
- is alive, in a way that defines, yet transcends, all other ways of being alive;
- is endowed with a ceaseless propensity for birthing forth new possibilities;
- thrives on the freedom to relate creatively;
- always transcends the rational cause-and-effect explanations;
- evolves as an unfolding narrative, probably without beginning or end;
- incorporates paradoxes which the human mind – at this stage of its

evolution – is largely incapable of comprehending;
- is transparent to the embrace of ultimate mystery; probably only the great mystics were capable of grasping this truth.

These features are the desires of the cosmos: an inbuilt orientation towards *wholeness, aliveness, novelty, freedom, creativity, imagination, story, paradox and spirituality*. These too are the unarticulated yearnings of everything in creation, realised in the formative blueprints of quarks and leptons, in the elegant patterns maturing into galaxies, planets and rocks, in the vibrational movement of air and water, in the digesting metamorphosis of earth and clay (it takes earthworms an estimated 500 years to create one square inch of top soil), in the photosynthetic nourishment of flowers and plants, in the playful passion of animals, and laterally in the self-reflexive consciousness of human beings. In the words of Carlos Castandea (quoted in Dyer 2004: 3): 'In the universe there is an immeasurable, indescribable force which shamans call intent, and absolutely everything that exists in the entire cosmos is attached to intent by a connecting link.'

Seeing through connection

Desire, or intent, is written all over the fabric of creation. It is the primordial driving force, always vibrant and creative, wild and generative; never tamed, never regulated, random but synchronistic, tangible, yet always mysterious. Yet, one enduring feature is manifest at every level: desire leads to union, not to division, to connection and not to separation.

No conversion, no change of heart, is greater than this: to come home once more to the desires of the heart, the desires born out of the womb of the universe itself, impregnated uniquely for us humans, in the planet we have inhabited for some 6,000,000 years. It is about time we came home to where we truly belong!

This patriarchal compulsion to divide and conquer is at the root of our immense alienation from the earth itself and ecozoic integrity. The soil, rocks, minerals, plants, animals, and even humans, are all identified in terms of what makes them different and separate from everything else. And in their isolated separation we then value them on a scale of their usefulness for humans. Despite the new understandings provided by the Gaia theory (Lovelock 1979; 1988; also, Turney 2003), we still persist in treating the earth as a fragmented set of disparate parts instead of regarding it as a great holon which thrives and flourishes through interdependent relationships.

Most serious of all is the fragmentation of the one planet into artificial political units we call *nation states*. When these are re-inforced by religious ideology, as in the case of the state of Israel and several Islamic states, then our addiction for divisive conquering has become unquestionably idolatrous. Now that we face the dissolution of the nation state (under the growing pressure of globalisation), we need to re-vision our relationship with planet earth using a different political philosophy. Thus far, there are few signs that we are embarking upon this new challenge.

Much of the division and rancour, the warfare and cruelty, that characterises humanity today arises from this distorted perception of the cosmos and the earth we inhabit. Our desire to colonise, to manipulate and control, to divide and separate, is a mode of desiring born out of ignorance of who we really are as cosmic, planetary creatures. It is a mode of being that is totally unsustainable. It alien-ates us deeply from our nourishing source, leaving us with addictive cravings that can never be fulfilled. We desire wrongly, because we perceive wrongly.

Seeing in a transformative way

> What we have gained by controlling the world as a collection of objects, we have lost in our capacity for intimacy in the com-munion of subjects.
>
> *Brian Swimme and Thomas Berry (1992)*

Reflecting on the discovery of relativity, Albert Einstein made the astute observation that everything had now changed except our way of seeing. And without that foundational conversion, it would take us a long time to behave according to the new relational principles that arise from the major scientific breakthroughs of the twentieth century. The change of heart is twofold: perceptual and practical. The transformation begins deep within, and translates into behaving differently, namely in a more co-operative and relational manner.

Sallie McFague (1997) provides a provocative insight that could enable us to see anew. Instead of relying so heavily on the eye, which we use consistently to analyse, quantify and 'capture' things for human use, we need to give *touch* a central place in our engage-ment with life. 'Touch,' she writes, 'is our closest sense; sight the most distant' (p. 71). Touch, she suggests, is not related to merely one organ, but to the whole body – and most importantly, 'I cannot touch without being touched' (p. 93).

This is the transformative mode through which deep rehabilitation takes place. In the networks of our belonging, where we really 'see' by *touching and being touched*, we begin to experience both the complexity and intimacy of the mystery within which we are held. From that primal base, we stand a better chance of honouring creation for what it really is, rather than from the perspective of it being merely an end for human means. Above all, we have some hope of befriending, in a more enlightened way, the great paradoxes through which everything in creation thrives. To that awesome topic we next turn our attention.

17

When Desire Can Honour Creation's Paradox

Desire has to negotiate both the light and the dark, the positive and negative energies which are innate to creation's evolution.

Evolution, from the originating moment, is characterised by the cyclic pattern of *creation and destruction*. Contrary to the denunciation of violence espoused by scholars like René Girard (1977; 1986), we need to re-imagine our understanding of creation's innate destructibility, acknowledging that violence belongs intimately to evolution's unfolding process at every level. Creation advances not just through progress but also through what we humans consider to be limitations and failures.

So, how should we read the violence that percolates through the whole of creation? How do we make spiritual sense out of the tsunami in the Indian Ocean that killed almost 250,000 people on 26 December 2004? Swimme and Berry (1992) strike me as the best contemporary scholars to have read the evidence in a wise and discerning way. Contrary to so many other theorists, they do not seek to get rid of the violence, and neither do they accept it as a fait accompli, in the face of which we feel powerless and all seems hopeless. They suggest that we are witnessing one of evolution's great paradoxes, perhaps the very one that throws light on several other paradoxes. And they name it as *the paradox of creation and destruction.*

Embracing paradox

The process can be depicted in a simple diagram with *(a)* indicating the upward movement I call creation, and *(b)* the downward movement named destruction. This is a universal process of a cyclic nature, perhaps best named as the cycle of *birth, death* and *rebirth.* New possibilities require a partial, and at times close to a total, destruction of the former life forms. To the rational observer, this will often seem random, mindless and meaningless. And frequently the new outbursts are not in obvious continuity with the old. To conditioned creatures like ourselves, this process often seems bewildering and bizarre.

To understand this process, and learn to live within its paradoxical embrace, is, perhaps, the greatest challenge facing the human species today. The key word here is *paradox.* What initially seems like a bizarre contradiction begins to make sense when we subject it to the wisdom and insight of creative intuition. To do this, we have to move beyond rational logic; much more difficult, we have to embrace the mind of the mystic.

In many of the great extinctions of the past 450 million years, the prevailing life-forms came close to total extinction. Sometimes up to 90 per cent of existing life-forms were eliminated. However, total extinction never happens. More bewildering still, it is just when we think that all hope has evaporated that we witness a fresh outburst. The new does not evolve from the old; often it erupts from some totally new source – dare we suggest the erotic power of evolution itself! This apparent lack of continuity is what makes the whole thing look so ridiculous to the rational mind.

Normally, we associate paradox with human experience and behaviour. This is a reductionistic view devoid of a larger and more illuminating context. Paradox belongs first and foremost to the story of the cosmos itself – the crucial point elucidated in the work of Swimme and Berry (1992). From the earliest moments of creation's unfolding story, life emerged through the delicate balance between matter and anti-matter, creation and destruction, life and death. Sophisticated equipment detecting events in the far reaches of outer space informs us that there is still an enormous amount of destruction taking place. Destruction is not the enemy, but rather the complement, of the creative process. Order and disorder, harmony and chaos, co-exist, as grandeur and new possibility unfold.

> ... the gift depends on a fine balance of two opposed qualities. The first is that the atmosphere and magnetic field surrounding earth are not so opaque as to conceal the light of the stars from us. The second is that they are not so thin as to allow cosmic rays to burn us up. The conditions necessary for human life and knowledge, including our star-gazing, myth-making, and metaphysical musings, are delicately balanced between the two atmospheric extremes of healthy opacity and lethal clarity. That dynamic equilibrium is, and always has been, a primary characteristic of Gaia's benevolence to the community of life on earth.
>
> *Anne Primavesi (2003)*

All the main religions, and patriarchal culture in general, depict destruction and disorder as a curse we need to get rid of. They see these negative forces as anomalies that do not belong to the plot as they understand it. Most humans accept this perception and endorse it fully. This might well be another of our great delusions, one that frustrates desire on a large scale, and consequently feeds the violence that ravages our world today.

The paradoxical dimensions of evolution reveal an incompleteness and irregularity to creation which is a precondition for evolution's possibility and progress. Without this paradox, everything would be fixed and rigid. There would be no freedom, no creativity and no capacity for desire. Contrary to what all the religions postulate, there would still be death, however. Death is not an evil, nor is it the consequence of sin. It is an integral and essential dimension of evolution's progressive story. Humans have major problems with death, and its often bizarre meaning, precisely because we are unable to befriend the paradox that characterises created life at every level.

What makes suffering tragic and death so meaningless is our deluded quality of human intervention. Because we are so out of tune with our cosmic and planetary origins, and with the paradoxical nature of universal life, we misread reality and abuse its desire to empower and liberate us (more on this topic in O'Murchu 2002: 94–109).

Rational scholarship feels the need for a rational version of everything in life. Things must be seen to work according to a certain logic, which we claim is foundational to reality and has been bestowed by the divine source of life. This is anthropocentrism in naked relief. This is human rationality betraying the foundational mystery and paradox that underpins creation. Here desire is abrogated and creation's desires tend to be ignored. Consequently, the seeds of desire which creation sows in all our hearts are also subverted.

Readjusting our desires

We need to make human desire congruent with cosmic desire. We must learn to live convivially within the organic spectrum in which all creation is alive (not merely humans and a few other organic creatures). We must learn to relate as creation relates, not in fierce competition but with intense co-operation. We must adopt the ordering of creation which consistently is one of holarchy and not of hierarchy. We must learn to befriend diversity and not homogenise it into human constructs that facilitate our addiction to absolute control. We must embrace the paradox of creation-and-destruction through which everything in creation thrives.

All our desires belong to creation's desires. If we fail to honour what creation longs for, if we set ourselves up as masters of everything else that exists, if we continue to exploit creation's resources for our own benefit, this is the surest way of *not* fulfilling our desires. On the contrary we will continue to plunge ourselves into the anomie, despair and nihilism which are reaching epidemic proportions in the modern world.

Creation has desires far more elegant and sophisticated than ours. While we continue to restrict the notion of desire to human feeling and behaviour, the true meaning and challenge of desire will elude all our research and exploration. Desire is not a human invention. It is a survival skill – and indeed a great deal more – which we have inherited from the cosmic womb and from our earthly planetary home. How to be more at home in the earth itself is the topic to which we now turn our attention.

18

The Desiring Fertility of the Nourishing Earth

The desire to be fruitful (fertile) is so basic that our ancient ancestors identified it as a primary quality of the Great Goddess.

> Every generation by virtue of being born into a historical con-
> tinuum, is burdened by the sins of the fathers as it is blessed with
> the deeds of the ancestors.
>
> *Hannah Arendt (1999)*

When it comes to our relationship with the living earth, the 'sins of the fathers' leave us fragmented and deranged. One set of desires predominates, advocating a mastery of subjugation and commodi-fication. Today, our living earth is widely regarded as dead inert matter, an object to be exploited and commodified at the whim of the highest and most powerful bidder. That is the strategy of patri-archal dominance, a brutal regime that mercilessly demolishes all before it for the sake of its own unquestioned hegemony.

A different view began to unfold in the 1970s, when James Lovelock, Lynn Margulis (and others) began to study the earth as a living organism. Their work culminated in *The Gaia Hypothesis* (see Lovelock 1979, 1988; Turney 2003). Noting several parallels with how living systems behave, it became all too obvious that the earth itself should be regarded and treated as an organic, living system. In the late 1990s an international gathering of world biologists in San Francisco elevated the hypothesis to the status of a theory. Although several biologists concur with this new understanding, biochemists and physicists in general frown upon this notion, and many openly ridicule it.

For the purposes of the present work – an understanding of desire in its planetary and cosmic essence – the Gaia theory offers several pregnant insights. But it feels more creative to explore those same insights through other sources, drawing particularly on the mythological and anthropological wisdom of ancestral times. While this material does not have the scientific depth and rigour of the Gaia theory – and will generate scepticism among some readers – it speaks powerfully to the peoples of Africa, South America and indigenous folks all over the planet. Their voices, too, need to be heard!

Re-earthing the Goddess

In our ancestral story I wish to revisit the Palaeolithic era (*c.* 40,000–10,000 BCE), one of the most innovative and original in our long evolutionary story. This is the era of Ice Age art when our ancient ancestors, throughout much (if not most) of the inhabited planet, indulged liberally in art, music and sculpture (see Mithen 2005). Creativity abounded, in what some now consider to have been a culture of celebratory joy and achievement. Virtually all commentators agree that fertility is the underlying theme of much Ice Age art. Several years ago, researchers suggested that the focus on fertility resulted from a widespread fear generated by scarcity of resources, especially food; nowadays most see it as an expression of ritualistic celebration throughout a long period of time when food and other resources were quite abundant.

For well over 100 years, scholars have debated the context and underlying motivation of this artistic flaring forth. Several questions arise around the recurring images of women in Ice Age art. One view that is difficult to establish according to objective criteria, but holds enormous mythic significance, is the belief in God as a Great Mother, which seems to have been widespread throughout this entire time. Contrary to the Sky-God which characterises all the major religions we know today, the Great Mother Goddess was embodied primarily in the earth. Indeed, the earth was typically regarded as her embodied, incarnational presence. And the fertility of the earth, its soil, water and other elements, was a primary expression of her prodigious fertility.[8]

The sensuous Goddess of ancient times

In this ancient, matristic culture, we encounter human desiring under a very different context. From the many studies on Ice Age art and the accompanying mythologies, we are gathering illuminating and provocative information. The art and mythology of Palaeolithic times (*c*. 40,000–10,000) suggest that sensuality and eroticism were freely and creatively expressed and that sexuality was a medium used to access and experience the power of the divine. Ancient art from both China and India liberally illustrate this trend, and the oldest world religion known to us, namely Hinduism, quite unashamedly depicts many of its Gods and Goddesses in voluptuous, sexual embrace.

For those who take the notion seriously (not necessarily literally), one of the surprising and complex discoveries is the sexualised identity of the Great Goddess. She tends to be depicted as a highly eroticised, flamboyant figure, portraying a conspicuously conscious pride in her body, and promoting the forward movement of creation through her prodigious fertility. Fertility here denotes not just the procreation of human life, but everything from stars to primroses, in prolific abundance. The tradition also depicts a dark, awesome and bewildering side to this strange figure: she can be fiercely protective of what she begets even at the price of consuming her own offspring rather than see it suffer unduly.

Whether or not humans ever actually believed in such a divine figurehead is an issue that need not worry us at this juncture – see the comprehensive review in *Feminist Theology* (Jan. 2005). Here we are moving in the realm of archetypal imagery rather than verifiable fact. We are exploring the deep search for meaning – the domain of primordial desire – that has characterised the human species for millennia. As Carol Christ (1997) indicates, some people regard the Goddess as a personality that can be invoked in prayer or ritual while others see her as nature itself, or the energy at work within nature; she is often regarded as a metaphor for the deepest aspect of the self. From a psychological point of view, one could argue that we are dealing solely with projections, based on fantasy and imagination gone wild. But there are few projections that don't have some depth of meaning to them, and many are loaded with intuition and insight which rational scholarship conveniently tends to ignore.[9]

All of which suggests that we humans have experienced ourselves as psychosexual creatures in a manner radically different from more recent times. It was sexuality itself – wild, exuberant, pleasurable, erotic and passionate – that made the Goddess so fertile. Through her sexual empowerment she could give birth to planets and bacteria alike. More importantly, perhaps, through her sexual playfulness everything she created was primed for pleasure and joy. Sexuality assumed two outstanding connotations:

1. it was a power for *creativity*, instigating and sustaining every form of creativity in creation;
2. it was deemed to be synonymous with *spirituality*, the spirit-power that constitutes the divine life itself, and all life begotten therefrom, revealed primarily in the erotic power of sexuality.

Paradoxically, and perhaps not surprisingly, desire in our time is pre-occupied with sexuality. Perhaps the allurement of sexuality today is a long-lost – more accurately, a long-suppressed – desire for an ancient wisdom, a wisdom brutally robbed from the human species and subjected to the crude biological reductionism of patriarchal culture.

> Cosmic consciousness and erotic human love in their natural state belong together … Love is a cosmological ray, given with creation, that arrives in spite of us and that we wrestle with in one way or another throughout our lives.
>
> *Veronica Goodchild (2001)*

The desire to be fertile

Carrette (2005: 27) compares productive sex with pleasure-intensity sex: 'If theology can move from an economy of production and desire to an economy of pleasure then it has the potential to make pleasure our salvation.' The former describes current practices and behaviours (technologies) whereby sexuality is commodified as an object of capitalistic exchange; the legitimate pleasures are usurped in order to make money.

Pleasure-intensity sex is envisaged as the strategy through which we can reclaim sexuality, honouring the more ancient and primordial significance of intimacy and spirituality; we then stand a much better chance of undermining the financial exploitation and cor-ruption of the sex drive. The fierce competitor can then give way to the intimate co-operator. Then, authentic psychosexual desire stands a much better chance of being truly honoured.

Several substantial issues, related to rehabilitation, coalesce at this point. The basic issue is the desire of the earth itself to be fertile and productive. Those who work the land, not just to make money, but for the sheer joy of doing so, know how pleasure-filling such activity is. Millions in today's world will never know such deep emotional and spiritual satisfaction. Even millions among farming communities no longer work the land; creatively aware of the earth's inherent biophilia, they are unable to connect meaningfully with this rich resource. This disconnection is the basis for a great deal of alienation, poignantly and tragically illustrated in the alarming rates of suicide among farmers in recent decades.[10]

Much more controversial is the suggestion that the fertility which endows our psychosexual propensities also belongs to the fertility of the earth itself. The eroticism of the earth and human eroticism come from one and the same intuition. This is first and foremost a psychic capacity to relate deeply and intimately. The first fruitfulness of earth and people is the pleasure of connecting more deeply and more fruitfully. In the case of humans, biological offspring is merely one outcome of this process. The fertility I allude to involves a great deal more than biological generativity.[11]

The desire to live fruitfully and with the satisfaction and joy of knowing that we make a difference is a legitimate aspiration long denied to the human species. And it is denied to us because we deny it to the living earth itself. When we reclaim our legitimate place as earthlings, and learn to honour all that earth is about – in itself, and for all its constituent creatures, including humans, desire can be honoured as God(dess) intended, and the long-overdue rehabilitation can take place. Then, we will know something of what it really means to live as fertile, fruitful creatures.

19

The Bioregional Connection for Desire

The earthy foundation of our desiring requires us to develop new ways in relating with the earth at regional level.

Essentially, home is a way of being in the world. We know we belong; we sense we have a 'right' to belong and, correspondingly, that we have something to contribute. We know we are welcome, and we feel a sense of being wanted, cherished, valued. And there is a deeply subconscious dimension that concerns us particularly in this book: *we desire to feel at home, because creation desires that for us.*

> The beauty of the earth is the first beauty. Millions of years before us the earth lived in wild elegance. Landscape is the first-born of creation. Sculpted with huge patience over millennia, landscape has enormous diversity of shape, presence and memory. There is poignancy in beholding the beauty of landscape … The ancient rhythms of the earth have insinuated themselves into the rhythms of the human heart. There is something in our clay nature that needs to continually experience this ancient, outer ease of the world. It helps us to remember who we are and why we are here.
>
> *John O'Donohue (2003: 42, 46)*

As creatures of the earth we desire to be grounded; that gives us the basic security, foundation and context from which we can grow, evolve and flourish. Without it, we may wander aimlessly for many years and feel deeply unhappy.

Structuring our grounding

The present chapter seeks to examine the context through which that grounding takes place. In the contemporary world, human grounding is envisaged primarily through the *nation state*, with supporting identities in terms of ethnicity, tribe, religion, and a socio-economic set of structures that regard the earth and the cosmos as inert matter to be exploited and commodified. Dividing the earth into nation states results in a planet fragmented according to the whim and fancy of controlling and dominating human beings, predominantly males. It is an anthropocentric form of division that has no congruence with either the earth or the cosmos. Whatever we may consider to be its practical usefulness, it is an alienating concept, born out of violence and essentially destructive for humanity and the planet alike.

In the closing decades of the twentieth century a serious alternative to the nation state evoked quite a wide interest, although little political or economic support. *Bioregionalism* suggests other ways of envisaging regional variation within the one earth, a construct small enough to facilitate familiarity and complex enough to honour diversity. The roots of bioregionalism go back to the 1930s when Frederic Clements and Victor Shelford developed the biome system of classification. *Biomes* refer to natural habitats such as grasslands, deserts, rainforests and coniferous forests shaped by climate. Particular soils, vegetation and animal life developed in each climate region in accordance with rainfall, temperature and weather patterns.[12]

Bioregional consciousness

The *bioregion* may be described as both a geographical terrain and a terrain of consciousness. It is a new and different way of conceptualising the human relationship with the earth and its resources. We invoke an alternative mode of relating based on a new way of thinking, facilitating a rehabilitation of genuine human desire. Kirkpatrick Sale (1991: 50ff.) identifies four central features of this new orientation:

Scale: Global socio-economic abstractions and intangibles give way to the here and now, the seen and the felt, the real and the known.

Economy: The cycle of production and exchange is determined primarily by the quality and quantity of local resources.

Polity: 'A bioregional polity would seek the diffusion of power, the decentralisation of institutions, with nothing done at a higher level than necessary, and all authority flowing upward incrementally from the smallest political unit to the largest' (Sale 1991: 94).

Society: Models of governance follow cellular principles in which families operate within neighbourhoods, neighbourhoods within communities, communities within cities, etc. Co-operation rather than competition, collaboration rather than conflicting interests, become the guiding norms.

Bioregional sustainability

Bioregions are far more integral to the biotic structure of the earth's ecosystem; nation states are false, destructive divisions, useful for those seeking power and domination, but of no enduring value for most of humanity. Bioregional grounding is much more likely to satisfy both our survival needs and our more enduring desires. It achieves these goals by maintaining our gaze on those sustainable values through which everything in creation thrives. Thomas Berry (1985) suggests the following as primary bioregional values:

- *Self-Emergence:* The earth is endowed with an innate power to bring forth those possibilities that enhance evolutionary growth and development. We, humans, need to adopt structures that will honour the rhythm and pace of the earth itself. We can begin with a selective replacement of those structures and technologies that are clearly deleterious to our progress. Examples that spring to mind include biocentric architecture, transportation and a more sustainable use of natural resources.
- *Self-Nourishing:* Earth is a highly fertile planet, drawing liberally on the nourishing potential of creation's chemistry, particularly the sun's energy mediated through the process of photosynthesis. And nature is incredibly adept at recycling waste so that nothing is ever wasted. A human species responsibly adjusted to the fertility of creation need never know hunger or starvation among its members.

- *Self-Propagating:* The earth's fertility begets new life in great variety and diversity. Contrary to the leading economic theories of our time which postulate *scarcity* as the prevailing fact (more in Long 2000: 144ff.; McFague 2001: 75ff.), prodigious fertility is one of earth's leading characteristics, paradoxically kept in balance by the unceasing cycle of birth–death–rebirth.
- *Self-Educating:* Ours is a wise creation, imbued with a quality of intelligence that defies much of our rational learning. This intelligent, autopoietic behaviour is elegantly illustrated in the Gaia theory (explained in Chapter 18 above). The self-educational process observed in the natural world forms a model for the human, one with which our ancient ancestors were often more acquainted than the highly educated folks of our time.
- *Self-Healing:* Currently, an estimated 60 per cent of all synthetic drugs used in health care are based on extracts from the plant life of the great tropical forests, just one reminder to us of a planet richly endowed with resources for our health and well-being. But in our current state of planetary ignorance, we are unable to adopt the convivial relationships through which nature could heal us and restore us to new life.
- *Self-Governing:* At every level of creation, an integral functional order exists within each regional life community; this is engaged and sustained by the interdependent and creative relationships that augment growth, fruitfulness, paradox and beauty. Few human institutions honour these organic principles.
- *Self-Fulfilling:* The earth community is fulfilled in each of its diverse embodiments, through the mutual capacity for co-operation and co-creation. In the human, the community celebrates itself in a reflective self-awareness; in us and through us creation grows in self-awareness. We contribute to this process, not through fierce competition or patriarchal domination, but through creative ritual, music, dance, song, poetry, literature, drama, painting, sculpture and architecture.

Think globally, act locally

In the contemporary world, the prevailing political systems fail to empower either people or creation. Commoditization is the ruling philosophy of capitalism. It has captivated the minds, hearts and desires of most people in the contemporary world. Not alone does it militate against alternative visions like those of bioregionalism, but much more seriously it jeopardises the deep desires of the human heart. Precisely for this reason, we need to conjure up alternatives, well aware that they will meet with ridicule and hostility on several fronts.

An earth-community, structured according to bioregional principles, invites us to a different quality of engagement, one far more promising for the rehabilitation of authentic desire. Here the principles of subsidiarity and participation can work in a truly democratic way. People will be happier, the earth itself will be saved a great deal of dangerous exploitation, and the giftedness of the cosmos will be more readily appreciated.

Rehabilitating a meaningful political engagement will require real local involvement in the restoration and recreation of viable local communities. Several examples have been studied and proposed (see Douthwaite 1998; Hines 2000; Suzuki 2002: 207ff.); some have worked well but unfortunately have not received the media attention and public profiling which they deserve. The worldwide web of information-communication provides several viable examples.[13] As indicated elsewhere in this book, the alternative strategy of *networking*, formulated by the United Nations in the later decades of the twentieth century, specifically through the restructuring of non-governmental organisations (NGOs), is already inspiring a range of alternative initiatives embracing the principles of bioregionalism outlined above.

Alternatives have been studied, tried and tested. We know they do work and can work. But we seem unable to make the quantum leap! Why? Because humanity's capacity for desire is distorted, undermined and disempowered. We are unable to choose that which is for our good because alien forces have been normalised and culturally sanctioned. All of us are displaced creatures, serrated from the cosmic womb of nurturance and hope. The rapidly growing plight of refugees is a symbolic statement, harshly embodied by the few (against their will) but reflecting a common plight of the whole human race.

The rehabilitation of desire is not just another psychological trip, or some type of pseudo-spiritual conversion. It is the precondition for the re-invention of culture in which humans, and all other creatures, can inhabit once more their God-given earthly home. The major implications are not merely social, psychological or spiritual – the position largely adopted by Farley (2005). Primarily, they are systemic, political and economic, as highlighted by Grey (2003). And we can no longer consign such responsibilities to the select few that represent us in political governance. They are no longer capable of representing us wisely – they, too, are out of tune with authentic desire!

Bioregional re-empowering, indigenous resourcing, and NGO-style global networking are three important features for the restoration of a viable earth, the reawakening of a liberated humanity, and the rehabilitation of the deepest desires that stir in all human hearts. Only when this larger cosmic and earthly context is duly honoured and integrated can we hope to do full justice to the call to become authentically human. To that topic we now turn our attention.

20

Befriending Desire as Embodied Creatures

Relating meaningfully as embodied creatures is foundational to authentic human desire.

Reconceptualising the earth in bioregional terms requires that we revisit the human body and its place in this new earthly context. To appreciate the desired bioregional reform for human living, we need to re-examine our perceptions of ourselves as embodied creatures. Beyond the commercialisation that usurps the body as a commodity, beyond conventional medicine which regards the body as a machine to be repaired, the human body displays very accurately the same dynamics and principles that sustain the earth body and underpin the potential for bioregional engagement.

> I am puzzled that a species that has subjected virtually the entire universe to its analytical gaze and that has penetrated to the tiniest constituents of matter still knows next to nothing about how to become human.
>
> *Walter Wink (2002)*

For some time now, we have known of other dynamics at work in the human body! Cellular biology opened up a new psychic maze of incredible elegance, complexity and intelligence: billions of cells co-creating interactively circulating through every bodily organ. Much more exciting is the growing awareness that the cellular world imitates the atomic structure through which creation at large unfolds and develops. The human body is the cosmic, planetary body in miniature (more in King 2004).

The desires of the human heart are the yearnings and longings that belong to the great cosmic web of life. Just as the language of mathematics cannot adequately describe the behaviour of atoms, so the standard descriptions of the cellular world fail to illuminate the empowering wisdom of the cell in action. Chopra (2004) illustrates how this wisdom works:

- *Higher purpose:* Cell-behaviour illuminates the principle of the whole being greater than the sum of the parts. Cells tend to operate for the benefit of the greater whole, and consequently will often sacrifice individual aggrandisement for the sake of the larger community of life. This is not logical, rational behaviour and it certainly is not mechanistic. A higher wisdom is at work, the autopoietic (self-organising) propensity that sustains everything in creation.[14]
- *Communion:* Although cells can be isolated, and identified individually by humans, in their own domain they always work in close harmony, communicate with enormous sophistication, and seem to appropriate their individual identity through their immersion in the greater whole.
- *Connectivity:* Healthy cells remain tied to their source no matter how many times they divide. In the laboratory, a muscle cell can be genetically transformed into a heart cell by going back to their common source. All cells are rooted in a shared common identity, a fundamental unity through which diversity (of function) thrives.
- *Awareness:* Cells behave with a distinctive sense of mindfulness. They know what's going on and can respond with incredible suppleness and subtlety. Their wisdom, whatever its source, outwits our human knowledge on a vast scale.
- *Interdependence:* Cells have been creating *networks* long before humans ever invented the concept. As Lynn Margulis (1995; 1998) highlights in her studies on the bacterial world, co-operation and not competition is the governing norm. Cells know that they need each other and work interdependently to reap maximum good for all, which seems to be the cosmic way of ensuring that deepest desires are appropriately met.
- *Creativity:* Although cells seem to have distinctive tasks related to the particular organ or part of the body in which they operate, they can adjust quickly and creatively as new need arises. For instance, a person can digest food never eaten before, think thoughts never

thought before, dance in a way never seen before. Creativity keeps us aligned with the new and, therefore, less susceptible to cling rigidly to the old.

- *Rhythm and flow:* Cells obey the universal pattern of rest and activity. Being compulsively active or obsessively aggressive are not options in the cellular world. Cells indicate that life at several levels thrives on cyclic rejuvenation. The cycle of birth–death–rebirth seems to be one of the most foundational. And in this context death is not evil, less so a consequence of sin. It is an integral dimension of life facilitating the unceasing process of creation and destruction, death and resurrection.

- *Sustainability:* Cells function with the smallest possible expenditure of energy. Typically a cell stores only three seconds of food and oxygen inside it, and trusts the environment to provide for its ongoing needs.

- *Generosity:* Cells expend their energy and vitality in building up living tissue for living organisms. They operate on the basis of an unstinting sense of generosity, which on closer observation becomes a form of mutual enrichment. This leads to a perception of creation as endowed with abundance, and not based on scarcity which is the underlying principle of capitalistic market forces.

- *Faith in the future:* Cells exhibit a sense of immortality. They reproduce and pass on what they can to future generations, yet they will self-sacrifice when the greater good requires it. It feels as if they know that the future is worth living and dying for.

These are the pillars of the *oikos* (house) where desire can see itself for what it truly is, where it knows an enduring sense of belonging. This is ecology in which desire is nurtured and sustained. When humans learn to live as creation lives and to thrive according to principles that are both cosmic and cellular, then we can befriend our deep desires in a much more authentic way. Then human contentment and genuine fulfilment are possible. Rehabilitation happens by natural necessity.

Embodied relationality

On the surface everybody seems to exist in isolation, autonomously, independently. Culture and society promote this popular perception. A brief reflection on our cellular make-up indicates that both within and without we are primed for *relationship*, not for isolation;

indeed, the capacity for relationality constitutes every fibre of our being and every yearning of our hearts. None of us can survive in isolation. It is our very nature to be connected and grounded. Our greatest survival skill is our capacity for relating.

Over the past 10,000 years we adopted a hierarchical, managerial, controlling way of relating. Many see this as a natural, advanced development from how we related at previous epochs of human evolution. It is becoming increasingly clear that we have lost a deeper, more ancient wisdom which is now coming back to haunt us. As rampant individualism reaps havoc, on ourselves and on the earth-body, the need to reclaim a more relational mode of existence becomes inescapable. In fact, it is one of the most urgent issues facing humanity today.

At this axial time, it is valuable to look back, not in fear, or insecurity, not in entrenchment, and certainly not in infantile regression, but to marshal deep ancient wisdom to enhance our leap forward. The past can be helpful to see what has worked well before, acknowledging that it will work differently in the new context. The story of evolution is a generic narrative, reminding us of the values that have sustained us in the past and are likely to enhance our progress for the future. *The human capacity to relate* is paramount among these values. Its rehabilitation for this precarious time is the subject I explore in the remaining chapters of Part Two of this book.

21

Desire Fulfilled in Meaningful Relationships

The rehabilitation of desire requires a radical redefining of our capacity for relationship.

> Relatedness is more vital than any consciousness and lies within it. A human being is first of all a being-in-relationship, then consciousness, then personal creativity.
>
> *Ivone Gebara (2002)*

Human identity today is caught in the conflicting strain of two major ideologies. The first dominant position owes its origin largely to classical Greek culture. Plato and Aristotle bequeathed to us an understanding of the human person that has prevailed over the past 2,500 years. To be authentically human we see ourselves as different from, and superior to, everything else in creation. Individuality, characterised by autonomy, self-reliance, independence and rationality, constitutes the essence of human nature and the heart of human identity. *Each person stands alone in his or her uniqueness.* The ability to achieve and maintain this sense of aloneness and independence is – according to this model – the goal of all growth and development.

This is also the understanding espoused by political economy and legal jurisprudence. Humans are first and foremost atomistic creatures, always regarded in their individual uniqueness, and assessed for their worth and value in terms of individual gift and talent. The survival of the fittest, although it has social and interpersonal dimensions, ultimately is based on each person displaying extra nerve and fortitude in making it for oneself.

An alternative paradigm

The other dominant view can be traced to more recent developments in the social sciences, but also it incorporates ancient insights from anthropology and palaeontology. It is encapsulated in the statement: *'I am at all times the sum of my relationships and that's what constitutes my identity.'* For many peoples in Africa and Latin America, and several indigenous groups around the world, this is their primary understanding of what it means to be human. The robust individualism we take so much for granted is alien to, and alienating for, many of our contemporaries. The relational model is, in fact, the one we have known and appropriated for most of our history as a human species.

Whereas the contemporary vocabulary of personhood is constructed around words like *autonomous, atomistic, self-reliant, rational*, the alternative paradigm is articulated with words like *relational, interdependent, holistic, process, intuitive*. Here we encounter two value-systems that are not easily reconciled. The latter emphasises the central role of relationality giving birth to and sustaining individual entities – fostering the diversity within the primordial unity – while the former claims that only individual entities are real, and relationships are merely devised to enable such entities to survive and thrive.

These two understandings cannot be meshed or integrated. One is essentially false, because it is not congruent with how creation operates, while the other evolves out of the relational dynamics that sustain everything in creation. One belongs to cosmic processes, the other is a man-made fabrication, a caricature so widely accepted as being normative, and even divinely sanctioned, that it will not be easily challenged or changed.

Limitations of a rights ethic

Throughout the latter half of the twentieth century the pursuit of human rights generated a great deal of research and activism. This was abetted by several pronouncements from religious bodies and church authorities. The catalyst in many cases was the United Nations Charter on Human Rights, promulgated in 1948. One can scarcely read through this declaration without being hit by the fact that millions in our world are deprived of basics rights like: adequate shelter, food, health care, education, basic love, care and protection. Even in the so-called developed West, basic rights to education, work and dignified standards of living are shown to be extensively lacking. Rights, and the freedoms that guarantee those rights, became the new preoccupation of the late twentieth century.

Like most cultural developments, the pursuit of human rights is characterised by light and shadow. The light is embraced in the desire to live with greater dignity and integrity. The shadow is the anthropocentric trap already highlighted in Part One; it includes the following features:

- It is assumed that humans alone have rights; in some cases this is extended to animals but never to the earth, or to the whole of creation.
- The pursuit of human rights is often presented as a carte blanche: to put it bluntly, humans can use and exploit whatever they wish in the rest of creation to obtain their legitimate rights.
- In several cases, the pursuit of rights became enmeshed in patriarchal governance. We note this in trade union activity all over the world. Unions tend to adopt the very structures and regimes they denounce so strongly. In biblical language, they seek new wine, while retaining an old wine-skin.
- A private/public dichotomy is adopted which is deeply alienating for person and planet alike. We see this in the concept of the right to private property, an objective strongly endorsed by many of the major religions.
- Rarely is the rhetoric around rights supplemented with the challenge to exercise respective *duties/responsibilities*. Without this complementarity the pursuit of rights can easily become another oppressive ideology.
- In more recent times, 'freedom' is a term often used in human-rights language, frequently with an ambiguous and confused meaning. Freedom from all constraint can be a prescription for anarchy, whereas 'freedom for' is the strategy that is much more likely to augment growth and fresh possibilities for people and planet alike.
- The single greatest deficiency in seeking human rights seems to be the lack of a relational context. The pursuit of rights tends to be individualistic whether in relation to persons or groups. And it is often adversarial and dualistic. Rights in one situation has implications for several other contexts; justice can only be

achieved and delivered within a strategy of collaboration and co-operation. (More on this topic in Bell 2001: 99ff.)

The right to care

McFague (1997: 40) distinguishes between a *rights ethic* and a *care ethic* (also, Held 2005; Walker 1997). The former she perceives as adversarial and negligent of the natural world, while the latter is based on the model of subjects-in-relationship. The rights ethic leads humans to regard themselves as the only subjects, causing them to seek the right to treat everything else in creation as an object, deemed to be inferior and subject to the whims and fancies of superior humans. Here, rights have become the deadly tools of humanly designed imperialism. Not alone is it disastrous for the natural world; it quickly translates into the powerful versus the less-powerful in terms of humans as well as all other organisms.

Fundamentally, *the right to care* underpins all other rights (see Wallace 2005: 96). A caring ethic immediately reminds us humans that we are not overlords and were never intended to be. Creation cares for us in our birthing and nurturance; we then need to care for one another and for all other life-forms so that everything in creation can function creatively and dynamically. Idealistic though it may seem, nothing short of this target will satisfy those desires that imbue the human heart and frequently become distorted and even perverted when we siphon off rights as if they applied only to humans.

Others may object that whatever the rights of the earth, we have to suspend them temporarily until we rectify the terrible imbalances that prevail in the human community today. But these imbalances are themselves the result of our ignorance about the earth and its resources. For example, we cannot guarantee the right for healthy drinking water to all humans until we address problems related to pollution and industrial waste, which in turn will require a review of how we usurp and exploit resources locally and internationally. All of which ultimately returns to the basic question: why do we treat the earth as an object in the first place? All human rights are inextricably linked to earth rights and cosmic rights (see the seminal work of Cormac Cullinan 2003). We either embrace the lot or basic rights will be deprived at every level.

And it takes a global context of this nature to illustrate the close link between *rights* and *duties*. In a sense, duties – understood as *responsibilities* – come first, and when these are exercised in an informed and conscientious way, then rights are guaranteed. When I espouse my duties and responsibilities as an interdependent creature within the cosmic and planetary web of life; when I respectfully acknowledge how dependent I am upon the giftedness of creation; when I appropriate responsibly and thoughtfully what I take from creation; when I remain continuously aware of those less well off than myself, then the fulfilment of legitimate needs stands a much better chance of being realised. And this is not merely a prescription for a utopian, idyllic world; it is the real world for a human community living out of a relational rather than functional understanding of what it means to be human.

An *ethic of care* reinforces the rehabilitation of desire. A culture of care is one where we prioritise our duties to love and protect all that guarantees a fruitful earth and a productive species. And our productivity is not just about monetary gain or material acquisition. As noted earlier, our erotic fertility is nourished and sustained primarily through relationships that connect us lovingly and meaningfully to the nourishing and sustaining womb of our cosmic and planetary existence.

22

Sexuality: The Desiring Energy of All Creation

Only when we honour the creative and spiritual power of sexuality can we attend appropriately to our desiring.

Of all the work that needs to be done to rehabilitate desire, none is more urgent than that of the desire for sex. In Part One, I outlined the lurid sexual fascination of our time and the repression that has accumulated because of the preoccupation with the biological function of human sexuality.

In order to rehabilitate sexual desire in a creative and constructive way, let's begin by reclaiming a long-lost wisdom. As a human species we have been sexual from the beginning of our evolution, some 6,000,000 years ago. While religious morality and medicalised psychology emphasise the wild, unruly instinct, which allegedly identifies us with our animal origins, little has been done to understand the cosmic and planetary factors that enrich sexual creativity.[15]

Sexuality as divine eroticism

In Chapter 18 above, I suggest that the Palaeolithic era (40,000–10,000 BCE) has been one of the most creative phases in our recent evolutionary history. Precisely because this was such a creative epoch, one in which humans all over the inhabited planet at the time liberally indulged in art, music and sculpture, we will assume that the spontaneous expression of desire was extensively honoured. And contrary to all the moralistic rhetoric about the primitive behaviour of our ancestors, the articulation of sexual desire throughout this long period is also likely to have been distinctive and illuminating.

Already in this book, I make allusions to the culture of the Great Earth Mother Goddess, a divine figure of exuberant sexuality, unashamedly erotic and sensuously embodied, at times in wild, uncontrollable passion. This was also the Goddess of prodigious fertility giving birth to the earth itself, to its stars, galaxies, planets and to the myriad life-forms we know today.

Here we touch into a mythological truth far deeper than objective historical fact. This is myth at the service of what Paul Ricoeur calls *the surplus of meaning.* In this analysis, intuition and imagination carry the day, and yet we do not condescend into wild fantasy or empty speculation. Evidence, then and now, substantiates not hard fact, but a great deal of intuitive insight.[16]

The Palaeolithic era depicts human sexuality with exuberance and flamboyant eroticism. There is not much evidence around for moralistic restraint on the one hand, nor feelings of shame on the other hand. Here sexuality is portrayed as a primary feature of the *divine life-force itself.* It is the eroticised elegance through which we begin to discern what the divine is about and how it functions in the midst of creation. Even Pope Benedict XV in his encyclical *Deus Caritas Est* (no. 3–8) acknowledges the positive dimensions I am highlighting here.

Most bewildering of all is the massive reversal of our internalised sexual oppression – the fear, the guilt, the biological reductionism, that have left so many emotionally scarred and sexually confused – all that seems to be notably absent in these prehistoric times.

Sexuality and spirituality

That our ancient ancestors identified sexuality with the essence of divinity is an intriguing notion. It is so much at variance with the anti-sexual polemic that characterises contemporary religion. It views sexuality as good, holy, something to be enjoyed and celebrated. But more than this, it suggests that the essence of the divine itself is characterised by sexual passion. In the desiring of the flesh are the very desires of God. It is in the depth of our sexual ecstasy that we experience the real energy of God's creativity.

We have so convinced ourselves that ancient cultures were primitive and barbaric, it sounds preposterous, in fact outrageous, to suggest that the peoples of Palaeolithic times understood that the divine energy was expressed and mediated through sexual eroticism. Consequently, sexuality was perceived as a *spiritual* force; it was not simply generated from the instinctual drives of humans but from the divine Spirit. Even in its wild, passionate drives, it exemplified the power and ecstasy of the divine. (More on this topic in Evola 1983.)

Not surprisingly, therefore, we have inherited, even to our own day, techniques for channelling sexual energy so that people could use those experiences as means of accessing mystical union with God. We find this in the Tantric and Kundalini traditions of the Far East. We have several ancient art monographs depicting voluptuous and exuberant sexual frenzy in what seems to have been the context of ritualised behaviour (see Mann and Lyle 1995). And, of course, Hinduism in its primordial expression depicts several of its Gods and Goddesses engaging in frolicsome sexual embrace.

Undoing distorted images

Throughout much of the Palaeolithic era, the *womb*, and not the *phallus*, was the dominant cultural metaphor. Sex, therefore, had a very different representational value: it served as an icon for the erotic desire of divine-becoming itself. For a start, it was not identi-fied with sexual organs, function and performance as typically happens in the lurid advertising and propaganda of our time. Sexuality seems to have been much more integrated in a creative and liberating way. The womb-symbol represents not a part of the body but the whole body, the body as an organism to be desired, celebrated, affirmed and proclaimed as a basis for new life and possibility.

And the feelings symbolised are those of inclusiveness, embrace, nurturance, intimacy and holding. It is a more gentle energy, yet powerful in its own way. Our phallic-driven desire for power, and the accompanying emphasis on biology and instinctual urge, is a rela-tively recent development, one that dishonours the bigger sexual story that is ours as a human species.

As a species, we need to outgrow the terrible suffocation of bio-logically driven sexuality (outlined in Chapters 5 and 6 above). It causes widespread trauma, hurt and unhappiness. Instead we need to re-appropriate an understanding of sexuality that is deeper, older and more authentically human. In its foundational meaning, human sexuality constitutes: (a) *an archetypal, creative force*, endowed with (b) *spiritualised energy*, and expressed primarily as *a power for relationship*. It is not about power *over*, but a power *with* – with other people, but also with other creatures and with creation in the totality of its earthly and cosmic existence. Our desire to relate, and our capacity to do so, is primordially a sexual endowment, always imbued with cosmic yearnings.

Psychosexual rehabilitation

> There is a secret bond between eroticism and absurdity. When nothing makes sense any longer, there remains instantaneous pleasure and its artifices. Eroticism is then a revenge not only on the insignificance of work, politics, and speech, but on the insignificance of sexuality itself.
>
> *Paul Ricoeur (1964)*

In the confusion of the present time, those who suggest that sex is at the root of all desiring are, in a sense, correct. The confusion I allude to probably belongs to the long oppressive history of patriarchal dominance and interference, in which male philosophy initially, and male-led medicine eventually, bequeathed to us a biologically determined understanding of sexuality, experienced from the male perspective as a battle to gain control over the unruly passions of self and other. In this context the 'other' came to be symbolised by the woman, as once more divisive and destructive power-games were acted out. In our time it has led to the highly speculative and cerebral portrayal of sexualised intimacy proposed by phenomenologists like Michel Foucault, Emmanuel Levinas and Roland Barthes. (More on this topic in Loughlin 2004.)

The work of rehabilitation is not about conceptual clarity, or the emphasis on ethical boundaries, important though these are in a time of widespread sexualised abuse. Rather the more urgent task is the retrieval of the deeper psychosexual story that characterises the human species, honouring both our psychic and spiritual make-up. When the deep story is reclaimed we can then proceed to articulate a more appropriate sexual ethic for our time. This is an onerous task, but one we cannot afford to abdicate. It touches the deepest layers of human meaning, love and growth; without this brave step forward, the desires of the heart remain grossly neglected.

23

Developmental Challenges of the New Sexuality

The erotic dimension needs to be integrated if psychosexual development is to nourish and sustain human desire.

Feminist writers are among the more imaginative purveyors of human sexuality in both its ancient and modern expressions. They name more accurately the deep yearnings rather than the superficial externalised behaviour. They don't begin with performance sex but with the power of the *erotic*. This is the underlying energy of human sexuality which the ancient Greek philosophers described as a cosmic power of harmony and life and which Plato described as the yearning of the human soul for union with the Divine.

Redeeming the erotic

In his first encyclical, *Deus Caritas Est* (January 2006), Pope Benedict XV acknowledges the need to reclaim and rehabilitate the notion of the erotic. This has been a recurring theme in the literature of the twentieth century, with C.S. Lewis (1960), Anders Nygren (1969) and the feminist scholar Audre Lorde (1989) offering some of the more intelligent, and at times contradictory, elucidations.

Adopting Lorde's insights, Carter Heyward (1989) describes the erotic as 'our embodied yearning for mutuality'. To speak of the erotic, or of God, is to speak of power in right relation. Sexuality, therefore, she describes as our embodied relational response to sacred/erotic power, a view explored in greater length by Paul Avis

(1989) and by the moral theologian Peter Black (2003), who provoca-
tively suggests that a more positive recognition of eros is what we
need to oust the eroticisation of power that prevails in our time.

Black (2003: 122) adopts eight features of the erotic, named by
the Jewish writer Mordechai Gafni:

(a) *intensity*, an antidote to superficiality and passive aggression;
(b) *pleasurable*, common to both the erotic and the experience of the
    holy;
(c) being present to the *infinity of the moment*;
(d) *the other as subject*, not object;
(e) *radical giving and receiving*;
(f) *the defining of self*, discovering the self through intimacy with the
    other;
(g) *overcoming alienation*, as each other opens up to the Other;
(h) *engagement of the creative imagination*.

Key dimensions

Four dimensions uniquely express how the erotic impinges upon our
daily lives, indicating once more what we need to rehabilitate if our
desires are to be honoured authentically:

* *Relationality:* Humans are designed (some scientists may say 'hard-
  wired') for relationality. The capacity to relate is innate and our
  whole growth process from birth to death depends upon its
  meaningful activation. Our capacity to relate is primarily through
  people (one of the most primal expressions being the
  mother–child bond), but it is also transpersonal in several significant senses, e.g. in the realm of embodiment.
* *Embodiment:* Our bodies are not just physical, physiological
  entities, randomly moving in space and time. Each of us was born
  out of the embodied context of our parents and from within the
  womb of our mothers. Our conception and pregnant growth
  belongs to a field-force of human fertility which in turn is influ-
  enced by field-forces in planet earth and throughout the cosmos.
  To live meaningfully we need interactive, embodied engagement
  with other creatures, human and non-human, but also with the
  planet and cosmos within which we live. Embodiment is the
  medium through which we live as interdependent planetary
  creatures.

- *Sacred/Divine:* As already indicated, Carter Heyward and Paul Avis identify the erotic with God (also Wendy Farley 2005: 101ff.). We are dealing with an energy-form that defies comprehension and, therefore, can never be fully explained. It embodies an allurement and intensity that yearns for ultimate union, not just with another person, but with all that is attractive in life in the full range of possibilities from atoms to bacteria, from fire-flies to persons, from landscapes to the stars that dot the night-sky. Sexuality, devoid of this spiritual and cosmic embrace, will always fail to satisfy.

- *Empowerment:* In the biological understanding of human sexuality the empowerment is confined to the procreation of new life. In the deeper understanding of sexuality outlined above, psycho-sexual empowerment embraces new horizons. These include the capacity to empower each other through affirming friendships, intimate mutuality, ecstatic fulfilment, enhancement of personal and interpersonal giftedness, passion for justice, commitment to right relations at every level of existence and fascination with divine engagement. We dis-empower each other, as well as life (and dare we suggest, God) when fear, moralism or sexual ignorance inhibits our capacity to relate.

Towards a new sexual ethic

We face a daunting task. Even to speak intelligently about sexuality is a frightening prospect for many people. Toxic secrecy, innuendo and vulgarity, misunderstandings and abuse, shame and guilt inhibit and pervert our God-given desire to relate in a mature, adult and responsive way. An enormous amount of restorative and healing work needs to take place. And massive re-education, particularly for adults, is a basic requirement to any breakthrough.

Much debate prevails around sexual education of children and teenagers. Much of it is heavily factual and biologically based. There is little formation in tenderness, care, intimacy and the development of skills in mutuality. It is also a gross contradiction that we should expect such formation to take place within educational settings where *competition* is a leading value.

At the other end of the life-spectrum is the gross neglect of the elderly. Psychosexual loneliness is widespread in this age group. If an older person seeks to articulate sexual desire, and explore its meaning, one is likely to be ridiculed on several fronts. We quickly forget that we remain sexual till the day we die; not alone is it reasonable, but indeed responsible, to explore ways and means to negotiate those needs.

In developmental terms, however, the greatest deficiency is in the realm of adult sexual growth. If we are to rehabilitate legitimate psychosexual desire in the adult population – empowering adults to deal skilfully with the psychosexual growth of youth – life-long educational structures, and a range of back-up services, need to be put in place. And this will save governments millions currently expended on the vast range of medical and psychological services needed to heal the damage caused by destructive sexualised behaviour, or on protracted law suits over separation and divorce.

Without such educational programmes and social-political resourcing, it is difficult to envisage humans becoming proactive in drawing up a new sexual ethic for our time. This is a complex undertaking, but one we can no longer shy away from. With honesty and transparency, we need to face the fact that sexual behaviour has outgrown the institution of marriage and the culturally sanctioned context of the monogamous heterosexual couple. Other cultural containers will be necessary for the future: some of these are already unfolding, e.g., more flexible and diverse partnerships; the suggestion that we reintroduce the notion of betrothal; rites of passage to celebrate sexual maturation in young people. Most urgent of all is the need for a more adult, mature discourse, devoid of the moralistic hang-ups of bygone days.

The rehabilitation I allude to requires a re-visioning of the entire sphere of psychosexual growth and expression. It needs to involve people from all walks of life, not just religionists and politicians. It may well be one of the gravest ethical and political challenges facing the human species in our time.

24

Erotic Desire and the Homosexual Experience

Sexual orientation suggests a sexual fluidity that can be embraced by wholesome desiring.

Everybody has an opinion on homosexuality and generally speaking those opinions are dualistically divided between those who readily accept it and those who are quick to denounce. Homosexuality also happens to be a thriving sub-culture, a lucrative business for some, a moral quagmire for several religious institutions, and at times quite a lonely world for lesbian–gay people themselves. What precisely are the desires being articulated in this orientation and how do we best strive to honour and integrate them?

Confusing evidence

In the homosexual world, desire is often equated with sexualised behaviour rather than with deeper psychosexual needs. This is evidenced in the deliberations on the aetiology of homosexuality which is quite externalised and offers little insight into the homosexual's internalised world. Since the literature is abundant on this subject, I will offer a very brief résumé of the leading theories.

It is claimed that some people are homosexual, and will be for life, because that is how their brain-activity is programmed. The internal biochemistry, genetic and hormonal structure, is such that they could not be otherwise. Therefore, there is intense research for the 'gay gene' and a handful of studies on siblings, especially among twins, show encouraging results. However, the samples are extremely small and scarcely justify some of the ensuing generalisations.

Evidence based on developmental growth strikes me as being far more credible, but wins little support either in the world of rational science or indeed in the lesbian–gay community itself. The addictive desire for hard evidence can be quite blinkered in what it deems to be credible information. The one-time Freudian suggestion that a homosexual orientation may be related to unfinished business from the oedipal stage, or from adolescent experience, still merits serious consideration provided, of course, that it does not lead to the automatic conclusion that a person is suffering from a disorder arising from a developmental malfunction.

In our heavily sexualised culture, youngsters, even in the pre-pubescent stage, indulge in sexual behaviour, often under intense peer pressure. Children and young people, especially during puberty and early adolescence, seem to work with a rather fluid sense of sexuality, and most entertain, however briefly, feelings and thoughts around a polymorphous sense of sexual identity. It is the impact of human culture, rather than biological determinism, that pushes most people in an exclusively heterosexual direction.

The suppressed evidence

Because of the toxic secrecy surrounding human sexuality, real life-stories are often suppressed and consigned to internalised oppression. I worked as a couples-counsellor for fifteen years, dealing mainly with heterosexual couples, either married or co-habiting. In this experiential context, it became all too clear to me that sexual orientation is not a fixed, hormonally determined phenomenon. Over those years I met many married persons trying to make sense of feelings around same-sex desires. Some rashly jumped to the conclusion that they were really homosexual and rapidly proceeded to break up an otherwise enriching marital relationship. More traumatic was the awareness of being a bisexual person, continuously taunted with the allegation of being sexually confused, leaving one feeling isolated and even rejected by significant others.

So much toxic secrecy! A lot of my time and energy was devoted to enabling couples to be more transparent with each other about what was really going on in the internal world. In many cases, we never even reached the point of mutual transparency. Little wonder our young people feel sexually confused and ambivalent! And what a debilitating experience it must be for parents who cannot communicate meaningfully on such significant issues not merely with their offspring, but with their life-long partners. Sexual desire is aborted and a great deal more besides!

Fixity or flexibility?

To honour our true selves, and especially our desiring as psychosexual people, I suggest the following should be included in a revamped psychosexual ethic:

- Sexual orientation is not a fixed commodity. Our sexuality is a form of erotic energy which is highly polymorphous – and has been for many thousands of years of human evolution. For most people it seems to follow a heterosexual path of unfolding; this may be due to the fact that biological determinants point it in that direction, and as several evolutionary biologists claim, it may also be the fruit of evolutionary development, viewed within a Darwinian perspective.
- The rigid division between heterosexuality and homosexuality is the product of a culture addicted to dualistic clarity. It is a clarity of the rational mind that fails to honour the developmental dynamics of the inner soul. For all of us the psychosexual life-journey probably carries elements of the bisexual space, and this is about a great deal more than biological preconditioning.
- While allowing for a preponderance of heterosexual culture, several people within that orientation, and many within long-term marital relationships, do experience a desire to connect homosexually. This seems a healthy and normal form of psychological growth, currently frowned upon by the dominant culture.
- Some people clearly identify with a homosexual condition as their life-long orientation. Human culture has known of gay and lesbian couples for several centuries and some of them have maintained life-long relationships. The allegation that homosexual relationships are more fickle and unreliable than heterosexual ones, is at least in part attributable to the hostility in the dominant culture towards any alternative mode of relating.
- Because of the cultural reluctance – and at times overt hostility – to view this polymorphous development in a more benign and enlightened way, abusive sexual behaviours flourish in our time.

Sexual dysfunctionality is on the increase, taking a heavy emotional toll on growing numbers of people, while sexually related addictions seem to be more widespread. We need a more holistic context if we hope to address these issues with greater insight and resolution.

- What are frequently considered to be deviant sexual behaviours, e.g., transvestitism (cross-dressing), s-m, etc., may also carry cultural meanings that merit a more nuanced interpretation (e.g., Carrette 2005). One notes, for example, that several cultures exhibit such patterns of unconventional behaviour: the native American berdache, the kathoey of Thailand, the xaniths of Oman, the hijras of India, the mahus of Polynesia and the hsiang ku of China. In all cases, these are regarded with a certain kind of spiritual respect, commonly attributed to a person endowed with shamanic capabilities.

Towards a new mutuality

Homosexuality can be the subject of moral indignation, lurid fascination, or cultural integration. It is not a new phenomenon, but has become a subject of intense speculation in our time. As a species we are unlikely to attain a more enlightened view while we pursue medical or biochemical explanations to the exclusion of other interpretations. I suggest homosexuality is not about the physical behaviour of two people of the same gender, but rather a cultural statement about each and every one of us.

Our human capacity to connect and love might be much better served if we adopt a less rigid view of sexual orientation. When all of us can entertain possibilities of being intimate with each other, and society has transcended its voyeuristic capacity for judging and condemning us, then I guess we will not become more promiscuous but more caring and loving. I also suspect we will become more sexually mature and, as a consequence, more courageous and determined to bring about a world of right relating where mutuality and justice can thrive.

25

Bringing Home Our Desires from Exile

Desiring has been undermined by the metaphor of Exile which now needs to be replaced with the metaphor of Homecoming.

Christian spirituality has consistently reminded us that we are effectively a people in exile. The notion arises from the alleged expulsion of the Jewish people from their chosen nation of Israel, and their resettlement in the land of Egypt. According to the Hebrew Scriptures the people longed to return to their homeland, but some historical commentators claim that conditions in Egypt were a great deal better than in Israel and that many refused to return when they were given the option.

So, what is the deeper truth of this prevailing myth? In the contemporary world, we know of millions of people brutally driven from the place they once knew as home. We also know of millions who have set up home in places other than the land of their birth. And in the mobility of contemporary life, substantial numbers live in different parts of the planet, sensing that the whole planet is home and not just one specific location.

Propaganda thrives on exile

The exilic metaphor needs thorough re-examination. The plight of millions of refugees and migrants in the contemporary world is the consequence of ideological divisions and exclusions put in place to safeguard the hegemony of the nation state. The goods of creation are usurped and controlled to the advantage of the few and therefore millions are forced into exile with accompanying poverty, marginalisation, starvation, exploitation, and frequently a premature, untimely death. Imperial rule (democratic or otherwise) offers little protection to most of Homo sapiens; rather it brutally betrays the very people it claims to serve.

The oppressive ideology that creates this nightmare is not entirely different from the religiosity of the Hebrew Scriptures. *Exile* became a major concern for the ruling patriarchs, rather than for the people themselves. The patriarchs could not exercise power or control over their own people while they remained in exile. And when they could no longer resolve that dilemma they began to postulate that God himself had gone into exile.

Preposterously, they claimed that God had abandoned the people, but, in fact, what they could not come to terms with was the realisation that they themselves could no longer exert power over those once under their control. Thus we evidence one of the great delusions of patriarchal governance: in trying to serve their own distorted desires, they grossly misinterpret people's authentic needs. And creation's needs suffer even a greater victimisation!

Much of the rhetoric about exile is a form of patriarchal propaganda. And the propaganda works, leaving most people feeling disenchanted, disempowered and disillusioned. To survive, many people opt out of mainstream systems and institutions. They opt for an alternative lifestyle, often paying a high price in terms of insecurity and misunderstanding among loved ones. As we move into the twenty-first century, this option for *alternatives* is likely to become much more normative. It is likely to be the first major step on the long journey home to a more authentic way of being true to oneself, and honouring desires and aspirations long neglected and suppressed.

The new metaphor: homecoming

Of all the spiritual metaphors we adopt today, I suggest none is so potent, timely and liberating as the metaphor of *homecoming*. The rich challenges of this focus I have briefly explored in a previous work (O'Murchu 2000). Before identifying the various dimensions of this homecoming, I need to lay to rest one major assumption, affirmed one way or another by all the religions: *human alienation comes from God.*

As the progeny of a God of unconditional love, human life, like every other aspect of creation, is foundationally beautiful, good and graced abundantly. Assuredly, we are not perfect and never have been. It seems to me that God has no problem whatever with our limitations, paltry and insignificant compared with the power of unconditional love. *It is impossible to be alienated from someone who loves us unconditionally.* No matter how sinful or rejecting we may be, unconditional love wins out in the end; it always does!

Consequently, the alienation we feel, the estrangement and emptiness that seems overwhelming at times, is not caused by God, and God has no redemptive solution for it, because it is not God's problem in the first place. *It is OUR problem*, self-propagated by deluded perceptions, particularly our irrational craving for power.

Our alienation is not from God, but rather from God's creation. That is the source of so much of our meaningless suffering: we are not at home in what is God's primary revelation to us: *the creation we inhabit.* And we are not at home in it because we have deluded ourselves into treating it as an object that we are forever seeking to divide and conquer. Once we face this dilemma, then we can begin to let go (repent) of our deluded past (especially the past 10,000 years), be humble enough to forgive ourselves, knowing that the God of unconditional love has already forgiven us, and redirect our gaze to the homecoming which now must be embraced with renewed fervour. We pick up the challenge in Part Three.

Conclusion to Part Two

The Need to Honour the Primordial Context

Desire, properly understood, belongs to the big context of creation and life. It is not merely a human propensity but rather the erotic, creative energy of the divine itself. And this creative energy becomes manifest first and foremost in cosmic and planetary creation, billions of years before humans first evolved.

We inherit our capacity for desire, not from some questionable psychic realm where the forces for good and evil battle it out for supremacy. That is a short-sighted anthropocentric view that has caused deep alienation in the human spirit. It cuts us off from the lifeline on which we are dependent for every aspect of our survival. And foundational to such survival, at least in terms of meaning, is the fulfilment of our God-given desires.

However, our basic problem regarding desire is not so much with God, but rather with God's creation. This is where the estrangement is felt most painfully. And this is where the rehabilitation needs to begin. Only in honouring creation's deep needs can we hope to reclaim the desires of the human heart. Spiritually, intellectually, politically and economically we need to develop whole new ways of relating to creation. None of these will be entirely new; we have related in these more egalitarian ways at previous stages of our evolutionary development. The know-how is etched deeply in our individual and collective psyches.

The work of rehabilitation, therefore, is twofold: (a) how to reclaim and reinstate ways of living that will honour creation's own desiring for erotic birthing; (b) how to outgrow the dysfunctional systems that dominate our lives today, corrupting and violating desire on an enormous scale. Daunting though the first challenge may seem, it is the second one that will test our wisdom and resilience. In our fear and confusion, we prefer to cling on to what we know, even when increasing numbers among us know it has outlived its usefulness.

The letting go will not be easy. Faced with such a formidable challenge we need to remember that evolution has brought us to such thresholds before and, despite our resistance, brought us across. Perhaps, more accurately, it has pushed us across, reminding us once more that creation's capacity for desire is greater than ours, and in that may rest our greatest hope for the rehabilitation that will guarantee a better and brighter future.

PART THREE

The Transformation of Desire

I think that every discovery of the world plunges us into jubilation, a radical amazement that tears apart the veil of triviality.

Dorothee Soelle (2001)

Introductory Note to Part Three

The corruption of desire, described in Part One, is in effect a perversion of power. In the patriarchal attempt to control desire, we have badly distorted its deep meaning and its potential for wholesome growth.

In Part Two, I begin by stating the obvious: we need to rehabilitate the legitimate place of desire in our personal lives and in our cultural values. And I go on to suggest that we can only do that by honouring and reclaiming the primordial nature of desire, not just as a human resource, but as a central dimension of all life, from the cosmos to the minutest creatures we know on earth.

In Part Three, I am inviting the reader into a kind of quantum leap. Instead of us trying to manage desire as suggested by Wendy Farley (2005), it seems to me, we need to allow desire to manage us. We need to adjust our whole way of living and being, so that it is congruent with the desires of the web of life within which everything is held and sustained. Let's put desire *in the driving seat and we become the passengers!*

This radical shift I seek to explore through the notion of transformation. *We become the beneficiaries of change rather than its activators. We cease battling with external forms and structures, and allow creation's transformative power to change us, along with the networks we co-create as social and political people. We surrender to a deeper wisdom, and thus are liberated for co-creative engagement.*

Christian writers may wish to draw inspiration from the story of the Transfiguration (Mark 9:2–9; Matt. 17:1–8; Luke 9:28–36), in which Jesus accompanies a close band of followers through a kind of mystical experience of reassurance and future-oriented promise. Rational explanation fails here (as many scholars indicate); wisdom seeps in from all sorts of unexpected places, and in unexpected ways. From a rational point of view everything is out of control, and Peter wants to cling on to the ecstasy by institutionalising it. At the end, the disciples are desperately trying to make sense of the experience. They know they have been through a paradigm shift, and how they wish they could make rational sense of it!

Desire defies rationality precisely by transforming it in the direction of the inexplicable mystery, the source of ultimate meaning. Only when we are transformed in accordance with our desires do we stand any chance of becoming creative beings for God and for God's creation. This is the challenge we seek to unravel in Part Three of this book.

26

Homecoming: A New Metaphor for Transformation

In coming home to God and to God's creation, we are transformed in the direction of what life desires for us and for our well-being.

Among the many things on which all the religions agree is the call to conversion and repentance. We need to outgrow the old way of life, typically described as the way of sin and rejection of God.

I suggest the call to conversion needs to be renamed. In all probability, our human imperfections are not of any great interest to God. This perception is based more on anthropocentric humans playing God, seeking to convert God so that 'He' will try to control wayward humans as the patriarchs of past and present wish to control them. It is easier to exert domination and control when people begin to feel shame, guilt and a sense of unworthiness. The patriarchal system seems unable to honour human vulnerability in a caring and nurturing way.

Conversion for our time

Conversion as a Christian concept – *metanoia* – is about removing the obstacles, the blocks and barriers that undermine our ability to engage with life, with the fullness of the gifts and resources with which we are all blessed. These obstacles are systemic rather than personal, related to perceptions rather than specific ways of behaving. And among the primary stumbling blocks is our dysfunctional relationship with the cosmos and with planet earth.

How we got all that wrong is explored in Parts One and Two above. *The foundational problem is our alienation from creation, our self-imposed exile from the homeland in which God has placed us.* As already intimated, we functioned well in this home for most of our time on earth. For the past 10,000 years – an era of patriarchal dominion – the organic, divinely inspired relationship has been badly disrupted – not by God, but by us!

This disruption has left many people feeling fearful and fretful. We feel nervous and uncertain. Paranoia drives many of our compulsive reactions, desperately trying to keep control, when, in truth, the only thing that is out of control is our very selves. We are the ones that are out of kilter, and because of our panic and paranoia creation is also in pain and anguish.

> Paranoia is a standard habit of the mind for citizens of the realm. The projection of the shadow of evil is woven particularly deeply into the rule of political life. Metanoia – turning around to face the darkness within the self, reclaiming our projections, and repenting of our self-righteousness – is an ongoing discipline of the spiritual life.
>
> *Sam Keen (1994)*

Now that we can name the problem in a more responsible way, let's stop blaming God for an 'imperfect' mess that God never created in the first place. Let's outgrow the escapist religiosity of seeking to elope from the vale of tears (which we ourselves have invented). Let's reclaim our primordial call to adulthood, and embrace the invitation to become co-creators once more with our co-creative God.

In a word, let's come home to where we truly belong and embrace the noble mission of developing and enhancing God's creation. *We have done it well for most of our time on this earth.* Instinctively and intuitively, we know how to do it well – provided we honour the deep desires that inform and illuminate wisdom in the human heart.

The journey home

Let's begin by delineating the stages we need to negotiate on the journey home from our self-imposed exile. These I have explored at greater length (cf. O'Murchu 2000: 89–124) and here I offer a brief overview:

- Embracing the horizon of belonging where the divine co-creator inspires our being and becoming, the realm where all beings are invited into co-creative participation. This is the sphere of cosmic creation, the elegant and fertile universe. The universe is the web of life to which we all belong and to which we owe everything that makes human life meaningful and productive.

- Planet earth is the dimension of the universe in which our existence is grounded. We need to make this our primary domicile, within which we access all we need to live in accordance with our divinely endowed purpose. Perhaps, the most serious challenge facing us as earthlings is to reclaim the earth-body as a living organism, cease from our gross manipulation and exploitation, and learn once more to befriend the organism that has so generously befriended us for over 6,000,000 years.

- And the homecoming envisaged in (a) and (b) above is not something we do in isolation, nor can we achieve it in the carved-up earth divided into nation states. We need to evolve a different way of social and political organisation, one that will respect *bioregional* mutuality and diversity. We will need to relearn co-operation and interdependence at several levels of existence. This will not be entirely new to us; this is how we have related as earth-based creatures for most of our evolutionary life-span of 6,000,000 years.

- The homecoming involves the appropriation of a new wisdom, with one outstanding feature: *everything in the alive creation thrives through relationality.* It is our relationships that define reality and confer identity. The lone ranger of post-modern individualism, whether construed personally or nationally, is an aberration in the relational network of universal life.

- And this means that we have to come home to new ways of organising our existence on the earth, not by propagating major *institutions*, whose agenda – overtly or covertly – is the perpetuation of their own power. These need to be replaced with evolving fluid and creative *networks* that empower both people and creation at large for the flowering and flourishing of diverse giftedness.

- Finally, we will need a revamped spirituality that can facilitate this new outlook with wisdom and discernment, one that procures depth as we seek to follow the Spirit who blows where she wills. While this spiritual fidelity partially lies deeply beneath the institutional layers of formal religion, it needs to be evoked afresh in each new era. The old can be accessed by a careful and creative reclaiming of the mystical wisdom of bygone times and of several indigenous cultures in the contemporary world. With such foundations, we can reconstruct a spiritual praxis to empower our homecoming – and home-making – within the inspiring and paradoxical creation which provides the ground of our being.

Churches and religions can facilitate and encourage this new endeavour, but experience suggests that the breakthrough will happen outside rather than within conventional institutions. We are dealing with new wine for which we need new wineskins. Yet, while many of the structures will be new, the underlying wisdom is deep and ancient. At the level of desire, we know how to be at home and, moreover, we know its transformative power. Once more the transformation prods and provokes us; let's hope we will have the vision and courage to assume the challenge.

27

When Desire Can Transcend the Decline of Patriarchy

To protect the integrity of our desiring, we need new skills to deal with the decline and disintegration of our major institutions.

One of the more formidable hurdles to be negotiated on the journey home from exile is that of the patriarchal system that underpins all our major institutions and informs our perceptions of reality. As indicated in previous chapters, I apply the term 'patriarchy' to the philosophy of divide and conquer which has characterised our approach to creation, and to each other, for possibly the last 10,000 years, buttressed by formal religion throughout the past 4,000 years. Its negative impact on over half our species, namely women and children, is well known; we are only beginning to take seriously its impact on the earth itself; we have yet to confront its defiant grip on the political, economic, religious and educational institutions of our time.

Out of control

In patriarchal terms, all desire is egotistical and selfish. In secular terms it is a survival instinct. For the religions it is tainted by original sin. It is something to be got rid of, and where that is not possible, it must be kept under strict control. Co-opting the insights of psychology, patriarchal governance has provided a range of therapeutic technologies to resolve the threatening nature of our desires. The drug

companies amass huge profits spawning on a contrived dysfunctionality which really belongs to the patriarchal system itself.

Desire cannot be subjected to rational evaluation, psychological
analysis, religious control, sociological framing or any form of struc-
tural manipulation exercised by the human will to power. Like the
Holy Spirit who blows where she wills, desire is fundamentally out
of human control.

Desire is a transformative process, activated and sustained by a
wisdom that transcends human rationality. It is a dynamic creative
energy that weaves patterns for meaning and growth that defy all
our human categories. It is a spiritual life-force that befriends those
of open heart and trusting disposition. Our desires mould us;
ultimately, we don't and we can't control them.

Befriending the breakdown

Patriarchal systems are already undergoing substantial transformation, but, in most cases, not by their own choice. This leaves us with
a landscape that at times is fearful, reactionary, chaotic and, for some,
utterly bewildering. Many people have already lost faith in major
institutions, and have literally walked away. We witness a growing
apathy regarding governance and voting; religious practice has seriously diminished especially in the West; faced with globalisation,
growing numbers turn to black-market practices. And the ensuing
frustration leads to massive increase in violence, but governments
refuse to look at the real cause of the violence. It is the exercise of
patriarchal power itself that incites most violence in our world today.

Those who govern try to listen, and occasionally modify structures to be more inclusive and empowering. Most times, it is too
little, too late. Modification will never bring about transformation.
The old system needs to die; we need to help it to die, instead of
trying to resuscitate it with cosmetic changes. In terms of honouring
deep desire, there is no way of escaping the dynamic of
birth–death–rebirth. It is written into the fabric of creation at every
level, and all our structures and institutions are subject to its impact.

All this is unpalatable to patriarchal governance. Clinging on
to the largely unconscious assumption that, like God, the patriarchs
themselves, and their artefacts, must live forever, diminution
and possible extinction are unthinkable. A core dimension of
desiring is not being honoured; transformation is being indefinitely
postponed – in theory, but not in fact, because transformative

breakthrough happens anyhow, with or without humans on board.

It is the stubborn resistance to change that is causing so much meaningless pain and suffering in today's world. Denial holds a terrible grip on our collective psyche. And with subdued imaginations – thanks to the influence of patriarchally infiltrated education – millions are confused and petrified. Even in the rich and powerful West, counselling services are inundated, while many other dis-illusioned souls resort to quick fixes to escape the evolutionary pain which characterises our time, the cultural impasse so aptly described by Moore (2004) and Sylvester and Klick (2004).

The transformation of desire, in this time as in any other, requires us to befriend the breakdown, not escape it, fix it, or rescue the dying organisation. The patriarchal system needs to die and, after that death, we will need to bury the dead. There can be no rebirth (Christian resurrection) without going through the parting, grieving and laying the dead to rest.

> In terms of facing these profound issues of survival, there are three learning aspects that we do not ordinarily identify with learning: the dynamics of denial, despair and grief.
>
> *Edmund O'Sullivan (2002)*

Empowering from the base

If we stand any chance of facing this dark hour with integrity and wisdom, if we wish to be included in the transformative process rather than engulfed by the alienation of excluding ourselves, we need to adopt other ways of being human in the world. Instead of looking to the power from on high, we have to reclaim mutual empowerment from the ground up. From now on it's not the head that governs the body; in more congruent organic terms, the body self-organises for the sake of the greater whole. Since we have few blueprints on how to do this, we will need to learn as we go along.

> Only through reconditioning ourselves bodily can the patriarchal pattern be counteracted. The whole body must take the lead, but with the enculturated big brain now chastened.
>
> *Bruce Wilshire (1998)*

We know that the cosmic and planetary bodies will support us in this endeavour. We carry the collective memory of having lived convivially within the earth system for most of our time on this planet. Indigenous peoples around the world, along with prophetic and mystical visionaries of our time, can provide valuable support and alternative models for living and organising. And the United Nations has proffered some alternative models for social and political engagement, the NGO (non-governmental organisation) being particularly relevant as a more viable alternative.

The NGO is modelled on the notion of *networking*. An extensive literature, and several encouraging experiments, support this notion (see www.en.wikipedia.org/wiki/Social_Networking). It emphasises the local over the global, fluidity over rigidity, the intimate rather than the impersonal and, above all, co-operation over competition. Throughout the long story of human evolution, the model has been tried and tested, and it has stood the test of time. Because it is the very antithesis of patriarchy, it has been shunned and demonised, but because it honours deep desiring, and facilitates the process of transformation as patriarchal systems can't do, it is capable of negotiating many of the major crises affecting humanity today.

Undoubtedly, it requires a massive change of heart, a conversion that will defy all our religious doctrines. Central to this conversion is the readiness to adopt a much more adult way of engaging with life. Patriarchal cultures thrive on parental models whereby the few govern the many and for that to happen, the majority have to remain obedient and subservient, which often translates into childish co-dependency. Whatever else the survival of the fittest means for our time, it will include a greater propensity to engage people in terms of adult maturity and integrity. The fuller implications I spell out in our next chapter.

28

Desiring to Reclaim Our Adult Selves

Desire as a human resource is particularly significant for the new sense of being adult evolving in our time.

The adult in our world is struggling to come of age. Our major institutions are inept at handling adult reality. And our educational systems, promoting capitalistic values for the greater part, do not prepare people to take their place in the world of genuine adulthood.

Consequently, the calling forth of the adult is either construed as a non-issue, because, allegedly, adulthood is already fostered and protected, or it is subverted as dangerous propaganda. Adult ways of relating require radical reform of the prevailing world order. Co-dependency needs to be replaced by interdependent living, subservience by equality, and patronising by liberation.

Pastoral care has to ensure that it is about empowering the adult to assume his or her rightful role in an adult way of functioning and relating. Caring agencies can all too easily fall for a form of remedial action that is disempowering rather than liberating. Particularly in a Christian context, we need to remember that we are about that fullness of life proclaimed by Jesus in the Gospels. That ideal must never be compromised.

Principles of adult learning

In a world where people are empowered to reclaim their adult selves, the following principles are of central importance:[17]

- Adults learn by doing, in a dynamic, interactive and co-operative endeavour in which educator and learner are equal partners.
- In adult learning, everybody is endowed with wisdom; both educator and learner have joint responsibility for the appropriation and use of wisdom, not merely the teacher or resource person.
- Adults opt for win-win rather than win/lose outcomes. For adults co-operation is more important than competition.
- Adults don't feel threatened by the success of others, nor do they measure their own performance in terms of other people's achievements.
- Adults tend not to be incapacitated by perfectionism. They are much more at home with soulful realism. They can live with 'good enough' outcomes.
- Adults relate with transparency from an inner centre of integrity, love and truth.
- Adults are in touch with their feelings and can mobilise their feelings without either wallowing in them or projecting them on to others.
- Adults empower by giving away their power and this does not leave them feeling weak or diminished.
- Adults who have cultivated soulfulness can tolerate and respect vulnerability, their own and that of others.
- In adult communication, we say what we mean and mean what we say.
- Adults address each other by first name, not by titles; invoking titles as a means of protecting respect, itself infantilises respect.
- Adults say 'thanks' when a good turn is rendered.
- Adults are people who have attained a mature capacity for relationships, with self, others, the planet and the universe. Such relationships include a healthy sense of self-sufficiency protecting adults from the abusive behaviours of co-dependency or excessive domination.

Reinstating adult wisdom

An exorbitant amount of time and energy, along with substantial financial resources, is invested in the education of children and young adults. From the earliest stages the system is competitive and unashamedly based on capitalistic values fostering a culture of winners and losers. The goal of our formal educational systems is not the purported development of the 'whole person' but the creation of a specialised functionary capable of maintaining and advancing our capitalistic lifestyle.

Even in the rich Western nations, when economic pressure looms, adult education is consistently a first victim. Adult education programmes are considered to be a privileged extra – for those that can afford it, for the elderly and retired, for those who pursue learning as a hobby or recreational activity. For instance, career breaks even when approved for serious health or personal reasons, are presumed to include education that will equip a person for future employment. In the public arena there is little or no recognition that adult learning could be a strategy with significant potential for personal and societal transformation.

Fear is the great barrier, but seldom named or recognised. A culture open to the education of adults as adults will have its standard expectations questioned and its social mores challenged. Adults who begin to think for themselves, and begin to act in more reflective ways, struggle to find a meaningful niche in the dysfunctional institutions of our time. In general, our dominant ways of living and behaving are not amenable to adult maturity; they are largely incapable of honouring adult desire, the cosmological implications of which are explored by Sahtouris (1998). In the business sector, co-dependent games of teasing, pleasing and seizing (power) absorb an enormous amount of creative energy.

Little wonder that restlessness, stress and a general lack of happiness are so prevalent in our world. Little wonder that alienation and estrangement are frequently recurring themes in spiritual and psychological literature. We tend to blame younger people for being so reckless. I suggest it would be more accurate and responsible to highlight the boredom and disillusionment that characterise huge sectors of our adult population. The cult of the body beautiful, seeking a perpetual state of youthfulness, is just one illustration of our disenchanted adult culture.

Young people today accommodate the post-modern culture with a measure of ease and comfort. It is our adults who struggle to make sense out of desire. Unable to transform desire in a creative and constructive way, we are left with several crises around adult self-image, adult usefulness, adult sexuality, adult faith and the serious lack of an adult spirituality. These are urgent issues sensationalised daily in the media, but rarely addressed in a seriously informed way.

Other forums are needed and for the greater part will need to be created by adults themselves. Social networks where people gather for informal sharings and facilitated programmes are a model to explore more extensively. In Western nations, retired people pioneer several valuable enterprises on life-long learning. Valuable though these examples are, they are grossly inadequate to meet a need of enormous and urgent import. To honour – and transform – authentic desire, the ongoing education of the adult population is an absolute priority for a more sane and humane world-order.

29

Discerning Desire in Deep Wisdom

To understand how desire functions we need to move beyond the rational and adopt an archetypal mode of understanding.

In Chapter 2 I briefly outlined the work of phenomenologists on the nature of desire. Although they explore desire in terms of attention to the various objects or goals we yearn for, all agree that desire can never be fully attained. And some theorists will acknowledge that this is a consequence of the spiritual essence of all desiring. None, however, plumb the greater depths that offer more comprehensive understandings. I allude particularly to the archetypal basis of human desiring.

Archetypal meaning

Desire tends to be categorised as an instinct which by definition denotes a force that tends to be primitive and disorderly. Much of our thinking on instincts is governed by Freudian psychology in which instincts constitute not merely the unruly aspects but also the inner drives that can beget deviancy and pathology of several types. This is a quite different understanding from the view of Carl G. Jung:

> The instincts are not vague and indefinite by nature but are specifically formed motive forces which, long before

there is any consciousness, and in spite of any degree of
consciousness later on, pursue their inherent goals.
Consequently, they form very close analogies to the
archetypes, so close in fact that there is good reason for
supposing that the archetypes are the unconscious images
of the instincts themselves, in other words, they are
patterns of instinctive behaviour. (*Collected Works*, Vol. 9,
quoted by Conforti 1999: 1)

The moralistic overload attached to the notion of instinct needs to
be complemented, perhaps replaced by, the more dynamic and
comprehensive concept of the *archetype*. The latter facilitates transformative growth while the former can jeopardise and even arrest
human unfolding.

For the uninitiated, *archetype* is a very difficult concept to com-
prehend. This is largely due to the literalism and functional thinking
in which we have been heavily indoctrinated. To grasp archetypal
meaning we need much imagination and the freedom to think
laterally. Let me attempt an explanation through a series of steps:

- *The creative vacuum:* This refers to the vast space that contains all
  the energy in cosmic creation. It has no known boundaries or
  limits. To the human eye space looks empty but in fact constitutes
  a vast range of sub-atomic particles and molecular structures. It is
  saturated with energy and from its 'emptiness' come all the forms
  and shapes we see in creation. For the purposes of the present
  work, it can also be considered the first context in which the
  capacity for desire unfolds.
- *Field influence:* Already in the late 1800s, scientists recognised that
  the energy of cosmic creation evolved in patterns they called
  fields, gravity and electro-magnetism being two of the better
  known. Fields exist everywhere, providing the context for other
  developments to take place. This tendency towards primordial
  structure to facilitate further growth is one of desire's most foundational elements, one that has long eluded scholars of every
  discipline.
- *Psychic blueprints/templates:* now we arrive at the notion of archetypes, constellations of meaning within fields, acting as attractors
  for new developments, strongly suggesting an innate intelligence
  that generates pattern and meaning in the evolution of creation.
  (More in Cole 2001: 72–7; Conforti 1999: 13–58; McTaggart 2001.)
- *Archetypes* cannot be known in themselves (especially by the

rational mind) but can be accessed in the imagination via myths, symbols, rituals, the arts, dreams and even projections. Hence, the proposal of James Hillman: 'First imagination, then perception; first fantasy, then reality.'

- For Carl G. Jung, all the archetypes carry numinous power. They bring about transformation, sometimes involving the collapse of one's conventional world view, and no small measure of darkness and confusion. All archetypes carry enormous light and darkness (shadow); paradox abounds in the archetypal realm, requiring deep wisdom and much discernment to decipher the emerging meaning.

> Archetypes are predispositions towards the formation of images, a priori powers of representation, in-built stirrings or lures that, if we can feel and follow them, will lead us into the depths of what we are and where we are going. They might be called messages-in-code, which we must decode and bring to our conscious awareness. It is difficult to speak about what these messages contain. Their general contents, Jung tells us, have to do with light and darkness, death and rebirth, wholeness, sacrifice and redemption. He saw such archetypes as the common seedbed of all religions.
>
> *Paul Knitter (1995)*

Archetypal desire

Psychologists suggest that we often confuse needs and wants. A craving for food (a want) may not be because of excessive hunger, but because I am attempting to fill up an inner emptiness, perhaps my need for love, affection, approval, etc. The *want* is a confused attempt to satisfy a *need*. The want is the external urge, while the need is the internal yearning.

Desire is about yearning, longing and wishing. It includes all those elements, yet transcends them all. Desire as an archetypal force represents that drive towards meaning that characterises the whole of creation. In human life, therefore, it tends to manifest in aspirations for advancement, growth, achievement and fulfilment. It yearns to connect and bring to realisation a reconciliation of differences so that mutuality through diversity can flourish.

At the archetypal level, we are effectively grounded in God's desiring for us; spirituality is inescapable. Our capacity for desire is the guide that leads us to co-create with the divine life-force. At the deep, primal level, our desire and the divine desire are in synchrony. The lure to a new and better future, in a creation often evolving through the birth pangs of the great paradox of creation-and-destruction, aligns divine and human desiring. What we desire is what God desires, despite the occasional banality of our human wishes.

Our desires, therefore, are to be befriended rather than controlled, contemplated rather than psychologically or philosophically analysed. The capacity for desire is the soul that animates the body, awakens the mind, and energises the spirit. Desire directs the will, not the will to power but the capacity to empower. Love, therefore, is the central element in all our desiring. And it is this same love that lures us in the companionship of all that is lovely in God and in God's creation. When we can trust that process, and entrust ourselves to it, then we will have honoured what desire is about, and however dimly, we will have known something of the transformation that desire exerts in every seeking heart.

We are called to discern our ability to flow with the ebb, to be ever ready to change, to listen deeply, and to be ever alert for the transformation that may shatter all our comfort zones as the Holy One leads us to new and daring horizons. An exciting call, but one that demands not just generosity of spirit but above all an alert mind and a discerning heart – two of the central features in the consciousness that we'll explore in the next chapter.

30

Desire and the Transformation of Consciousness

Consciousness describes the deep wisdom that prevails through-out all creation, mediated strongly in our capacity for desire.

When desire becomes identified with a particular object, or even with one distinctive set of behaviours, then automatically we have distorted desire, stymied its flow and jeopardised its creative energy. Desire belongs more integrally and innately to the realm of spirit, and impacts strongly on the consciousness that influences our daily behaviour.

In the prevailing wisdom of our time, not alone have we distorted the fundamental meaning of desire, but we have also undermined the meaning of consciousness. Most scholars associate consciousness with specific behaviours of the human brain and with mental functions that operate therein. Daniel Dennett (1992), adopting an extremely mechanistic understanding, but one shared by many scholars, postulates that consciousness consists of tiny atom-like units called 'qualia' that can be observed, measured and quantified as we do with any other object under human evaluation.

Consciousness and the body

As a hotly debated issue of our time, three strands of exploration can be noted in consciousness studies. The first and most prevalent – in the West and specifically among academics – is the mechanistic understanding referred to above; consciousness is a form of neural brain activity focused on the interactive behaviour of qualia.

The second realm belongs mainly to psychology, often differentiating between what happens in the brain and in the mind. Consciousness tends to be associated with the mind rather than with the brain, and is perceived to influence all our behaviour and not just brain activity.

The third strand is very much a minority position occupied by those who consider consciousness as a property of all created reality, informing and infusing matter throughout the universe. The mystics of all ages and religions endorse this view and so do a small number of contemporary scientists and theologians.

> For matter acts as if it has consciousness, and consciousness itself appears to reach deeply into the structure of matter.
> *Veronica Goodchild (2001)*

In the present work, I adopt the third option but with the qualification that consciousness is closely identified with embodiment rather than with something less tangible such as mind or soul. It seems to me that consciousness describes that quality of awareness through which we relate as embodied creatures with all other embodied organisms, from bacteria to the cosmos at large. The body is the process through which we channel the wisdom that enables us to grow, develop, engage with life and realise our distinctive potentials. This quality of wisdom I equate with consciousness.

Studying consciousness today

The study of consciousness features increasingly in scientific research. With the development of quantum physics in the twentieth century a great deal of attention focused on how human thought could influence experiential outcomes, suggesting that our perceptions of reality are our way of bringing things into being. This is broadly known as the Copenhagen interpretation which states that there is no objective reality, only that which we create through the power of thought, perception and intention. We participate in a process of co-creation, with the emphasis very much on we, humans, being the main inventors.

Not all quantum physicists accept this interpretation and in more recent decades there seems to be a move away from its anthropocentric simplicity. That we participate in a consciously informed creative process is a notion very much in vogue, with a slow but gradual acknowledgement that the alluring wisdom is not primarily, or exclusively, with humans but with cosmic creation at large. In other words, we desire to act wisely because creation endows us with this propensity.

This approach commences with the notion that the dualistic division between matter and consciousness no longer stands up to scientific scrutiny. It is, therefore, more creative and, dare I suggest, more responsible to 'start with consciousness or mind itself as to what is most real and foundational in the universe, and work from consciousness to the material world' (Terence L. Nicholas 2003: 160).

Although only a minority view, it has gained in popularity and in credibility throughout the latter half of the twentieth century. Matter is concentrated energy. Human thought is also a form of energy. Do both channels – material reality and human thought process – arise from a deeper substratum? And how deep must we delve before finding a coherent explanation for the desires that imbue and inform our human consciousness?

The landscape of consciousness

Jean Gebser (1986/1949) identifies five structures in the evolution of consciousness and these he traces through the historical emergence of the human species. Adopting the same namings, I wish to propose that they belong primordially not to the human, but to the cosmic and planetary realms of creation.

- *The Archaic.* In human terms, this is the phase of deep unconscious bonding between humans and nature. Allegedly self-awareness is totally lacking – a view I do not share. Rather than identified as one particular time-phase, I suggest we view this as an experiential stage – a mystic-type integration with the natural world – known to all humans, ancient and modern, one in which current Westerners are quite deficient. Perhaps only contemporary mystics can integrate this deep earth-spirit synthesis.
- *The Magical.* Belonging largely to the pre-linguistic stage of human evolution, the magical represents the playfulness with which humans interacted with their environment, negotiating major transitions mainly through ritual-making. In our time, the ritual-

maker is a threatened species, usurped by the liturgist, priest, imam, etc., while the transformed consciousness facilitated by creative rituals is one of the greatest deficiencies of our age.

- *The Mythical.* This stage reminds us of the capacity for story-telling through which we weave identity and unity from within the fabric of cosmic-planetary life. Deprived of the narrative infrastructure in our time (stories tend to be reserved for children), we lack connection with the interweaving through which creation operates, and the co-operative role we are invited to play therein.

- *The Mental.* Here we need to distinguish mind from brain. The human brain provides the physical and neurological basis for the wholesome functioning of the human body, but the intelligence behind that entire operation is not confined to the brain. It belongs to the entire body as an open-system interacting with the enveloping body of planet earth and the cosmos at large. 'Mental' is a naming for intelligence, but redefined in terms of the larger landscape through which all creation functions intelligibly.

- *The Integral.* The goal of all evolution, as Teilhard de Chardin intimated many years ago, is to attain Omega consciousness. Christians tend to identify this with eternal life in Heaven. In contemporary theology I suggest we link it to some of the emerging insights on our understanding of the Holy Spirit.

Consciousness and transformation

Consciousness describes the deeper wisdom through which everything in creation is begotten and thrives. It is the oldest wisdom known to life and nature. Theologian Denis Edwards (2004) suggests that the Big Bang itself is the work of the Holy Spirit of God, an energising, inspiring, liberating force that imbues every aspect of creation from time immemorial, vividly described by Mark Wallace (2005: 7) as 'The Spirit is not a heavenly phantom – immaterial and unreal – but God's all pervasive presence and energy within the universe.'

Most scientists would baulk at my rather sudden introduction of a religious and theological concept. Adopting such interdisciplinary insights is not merely desirable but, in my opinion, essential, if we are to honour the complex nature of human desiring and the transformative impact consciousness exerts on our capacity for desire.

From a human point of view, consciousness includes yet transcends all our knowledge and information. As beneficiaries of a wise universe we are never at a loss. Unfortunately right now we are losing-out big time, because we no longer know how to access this universal field of wisdom. As in-spirited, spiritualised people we are disconnected from our ancient spiritual rootedness.

Retrieving this subverted wisdom will not come easily to Homo sapiens. It demands that we let go of all the anthropocentric props and dogmas, that we shed our addiction to power and control, that we surrender and become humble once more! The pathway of transformation requires no less of us! Then from that paradoxical position of apparent powerlessness and helplessness, we regain our lost freedom and we rediscover authentic rather than fabricated desire. But not without going through the proverbial dark night, the subject I review in the next chapter.

31

Transforming Desire in the Dark Night

Even in times of darkness and confusion, desire is fully at work; without the paradox of light and darkness, it cannot be honoured.

We humans have been indoctrinated in an ideology of control. Our felt need to be totally in charge is an unnamed compulsion that catapults us into a great deal of anguish, alienation, reaction and disconnection from authentic desire. It also leaves us with a false sense of perfectionism, whereby we expect life to run smoothly all the time – according to our preconceived plan. If nature were totally accommodated to such wishes, creation would have ceased millions of years ago.

Evolution thrives on restlessness, untidiness and incompleteness. At times, it feels as if everything is out of control. At times like these, it can be counterproductive to try and get rid of the chaos and confusion; instead we need to embrace them and contemplatively discern the underlying wisdom. And to assist us in this task, we can reclaim a recurring theme in all the great mystical traditions: *the dark night of the soul.*

The metaphorical dark night belongs innately to every transformative experience, personal, social, planetary or cosmic. This is the great paradox I have referred to many times in this book. It is unavoidable. Moreover, it is not some bizarre dilemma that has to be endured so that things can get back to normal. No, it has to be embraced, and in embracing it, we begin to realise that it belongs integrally to the pursuit of 'normalcy'.

Embracing our dark night

There are several dimensions to the cultural dark night of our time. The aspect we tend to deny most is the very one we need to face urgently. In the grim prognosis of Leakey and Lewin (1996), we humans are staring extinction in the face, but nobody wants to look reality in the eye. We ourselves have become the *Sixth Extinction*! We have diminished and even eliminated several other life-forms, some on a global scale. We have scarcely begun to face that murderous, violent side of ourselves.

If we want to be part of the transformation I describe, we must engage with this crisis – proactively rather than in morbid despair. For one thing, we have been through mass extinctions before, and we have survived, admittedly with drastically changed perceptions of how things function in our world. This time round, things are different: *the whole race is participating in this crisis*. This is a global desert moment, and the negative impact is likely to be cumulative rather than partial. However, we can appropriate and embrace the crisis within different levels of meaning, ones that can honour rather than subvert deep desire. This is a dark night that can overwhelm us; it is also one we can embrace, and precisely in that surrender, we can see a way through.

> [Apophatic theology is] speech about God which is the failure of speech; it is failure in the sense of speech slowing to a halt in awed wonder before the presence of what is always more than one can say.
>
> *Denys Turner (1995a)*

Of course, this option requires enormous faith and vision, and these are not in abundant supply at this time. The 'faith' I refer to is a spiritual resource (not necessarily a religious one) and it is capable of embracing many facets of our life experience. It also engages our deep story, not one in which we regress into an idyllic past and romanticise our grief and anguish, but a past that can be culturally and spiritually reclaimed to resource us for the difficult evolutionary transitions we face today. On this note John Stewart (2000: 233) reminds us:

For most of the last 100,000 years up until about 10,000 years ago, humans lived as foragers in small multi-family cooperative bands of a few tens of people. These bands were typically linked into cooperative tribal societies of a few hundred or a few thousand people. The bands within a tribe met regularly and shared common beliefs and cultural backgrounds. Individuals could move between bands, but only if the bands were within the one tribe. Inculcated moral codes and social norms that were passed from generation to generation controlled the behaviour of the people within bands and within each tribe to produce cooperative organisation. And the codes also organised members of the group to punish any individuals who broke the codes. Unlike the more complex hierarchical human societies that began to emerge about 10,000 years ago, powerful kings or rulers did not govern the earlier bands and tribes. *External management played no role in the organisation of cooperation.* A distinctive feature of the codes and norms that organised these tribal societies is that they tended to produce egalitarian behaviour. (Emphasis mine)

Negotiating our way in the dark

The dark night we face requires above all else the abandonment of the patriarchal desire to divide and conquer. It is our compulsive addiction to power that is destroying humanity today and badly damaging the earth we inhabit. And the addiction to power begets a vast range of other addictions, around money, drugs, sex, gambling, hedonism, individualism, etc. We tend to interpret these as personal deficiencies caused by sin or selfishness. In several cases, they represent attempts at compensating for our lack of a meaningful spirituality and an integrated mysticism. Our souls have been so parched by the rationalism and functionalism of patriarchal governance that we are starving for a quality of experience that will honour our deep desiring. Inadvertently, we opt for resolutions that exacerbate our pain and suffering, because we lack the wisdom to do otherwise.

Bruce Wilshire (1998) captivates the dilemma when he describes the mechanistic culture pushing buttons and turning dials, or recruiting auxiliary care-givers, while all the time undermining the development of skills and talents that would nourish the satisfaction of primal needs. Disconnected from our bodily needs, and estranged from the processes of nature, we ache and hunger for meaning. Disconnection from nature, in the name, ironically, of natural science leaves a bottomless pit. Addictive behaviours pour into it.

> But awe in the face of the universe, and gratitude at being a small part of it – awe and gratitude that are not merely momentary – eat away at addictions ... awe undermines addictions.
>
> *Bruce Wilshire (1998)*

Repairing the damage done, altering the existing structures (often on the assumption that we really can't do without them), or the more radical strategy of deconstruction are all largely a waste of time. The old edifices of power, the constructs that uphold domination, resist any effort at reform. The more powerful they are, the more they will feel the threat of those who disagree with their way of doing things. Resistance and defensiveness become predictable responses while those who challenge their hegemony are sure to be scapegoated. The way forward, as in all great cultural transitions, is not that of reform, but that of *transformation* (see Wilshire 1998: 257–8). Can we allow evolution itself to forge a new synthesis? This becomes the central question in the transformative process.

Transformation in the dark

Transformation does not come easy, not because we are incapable or even incompetent, in terms of understanding its dynamics, but rather because we choose to undermine (and often destroy) the very foundations of our existence as cosmic, planetary creatures. We have turned ourselves into mindless robots and that is how we behave most of the time, addicted to the lure of consumerism. And all the major institutions we have put in place to serve our needs and feed our desires are also the product of the same misguided process.

We expend an enormous amount of energy and vitality on minimalism; in a sense this is the desert experience of our time. Our world view is based on a very congested narrative. Most of our species have no sense at all of the real story. Our formative processes and educational systems largely ignore the fact that we have been on this earth for 6,000,000 years, and that the proactive creativity of cosmic, planetary and spirit-infused life has been fully at work in us throughout all that time. Those who govern, educate and lead tend to dismiss most of the story as primitive, barbaric, pagan, pre-rational, pre-logical, etc. And then we wonder why anomie and alienation take such a heavy toll on our living spirits!

Even our spirituality can be co-opted in sophisticated texts and theories imbued with time-honoured significance. Mystical authors like Turner (1995a) describe in great detail the darkness of God, that brand of spiritual emptiness and felt sense of divine absence described as apophatic mysticism. One wonders how much of this belongs to a type of self-perpetuated estrangement based not on an absence of God but on the alienation that ensues when we are not appropriately rooted in God's creation. More positively, perhaps what the mystic is experiencing is a mirror image of the human condition when it becomes grossly disconnected from the earth and from the cosmos. Even in our spiritual discourse we run the risk of rationalising the mystery itself.

Transformation, on the other hand, is a rather elusive term, mainly because it cannot be subjected to rational analysis or managerial skill. Transformation is not something humans invent, manage or control but rather something to which we surrender. How we dread that word *surrender*! It makes us feel powerless, passive and, most seriously of all, it questions our felt need to be in charge and in control. And the prevailing religiosity in the contemporary world complicates matters further: if we surrender, to whom or what are we surrendering? Might this not be another ploy to allure us into evil or satanic forces? This is where the big picture becomes critically important.

The *via transformativa* (way of transformation) belongs primarily to the story of cosmic creation, the contours of which I have already outlined in this book. Creation unfolds unceasingly through the chaotic but creative paradox of regeneration-and-destruction. With this paradoxical mixture the living Spirit weaves and moulds the raw stuff of creation, birthing forth the dazzling array of cosmic, planetary and organic life that adorns the landscape of our existence. From a human point of view it is full of contradiction, paradox, mystery and elegance. As human creatures, we are an integral dimension of this process, but we are not in charge, not even in the minutest way!

Transformation works to our advantage when we learn to flow with its evolving process, contemplate its vastness, trust its mystique, befriend its paradoxes, surrender to its wisdom and, finally, co-create with its deepest desire for the birthing of new possibilities! It is on this latter point that humanity proves a viable species or not. If we learn to co-operate with this cosmic creative process then we also become its beneficiaries. If we fail to do so, creation will one day get rid of us and replace us with a more seemly species. All of which sounds capricious and outrageous to the civilised intellect of our modern world, a quality of intelligence which sadly has not kept pace with the intelligence of the larger creation.

> Many people claim to have integrated their shadow sides, but that effort is itself a work against the dark. To integrate it is to co-opt it into the light. The real task is to live in, and with the darkness, appreciating its unredeemed value and loving its irreversible qualities. What is needed is a view of life that includes the dark ... It is the pulling apart of meaning so that mystery can be revealed.
>
> *Thomas Moore (2004)*

Transformation embraces many dynamics that simply fail to make sense to the rational human mind. It requires a quality of imagination, intuition, risk and paradox which are in short supply in our rational world. But as the crisis deepens for Homo sapiens, *and deepen it will as we move further into the twenty-first century*, we may surprise even ourselves by the adjustments we will make. Under pressure, humanity becomes an incredibly resilient species – perhaps another reminder that in the end we are transparent and receptive to the power of transformation.

32

Desire and the Mystic's Yearning

Desire transgresses boundaries that defy rational explanation; the wisdom of the great mystical traditions illuminates what's happening.

It may seem more logical to situate reflections on *mysticism* after the chapter on *consciousness*. I have deliberately placed in the intervening space the reflections on the *dark night*. As the biographies of many great mystics indicate, the dark is never far away in the mystical experience. In fact, it is the readiness and ability to befriend the dark, and not evade it, that authenticates the mystic's endeavour.

Mysticism haunts the human imagination. The topic is never too far from the investigative eye, yet all the formal religions exhibit a beleaguered ambivalence, often pushing the mystic to the margins of irrelevancy. Every generation pioneers a new spate of research and writing on the subject. And the more we delve into its depths, the more there awaits our discernment.

The mystical yearning

> The most heartfelt desire, at least in those men whose desires are not curtailed by natural necessity, is the desire not to die, to live forever: this indeed is man's highest and ultimate desire, the desire of all desires.
>
> *Ludwig Feuerbach (2004)*

In a sense Feuerbach is right! A desire for the infinite imbues the deepest recesses of our beings, and thankfully modern science has come to acknowledge and affirm this deep cosmic and planetary yearning. At a conscious level we want to live forever; we want to be immortal – perhaps more of a male than female preoccupation, as several feminist scholars note. In the Genesis myth of the Hebrew Scriptures, we are told that humans wanted to become like Gods. It is often depicted as the great sin of pride, the superior vice in patriarchal cultures.

Why do we want to become like Gods? The mystic provides probably the most authentic of all responses: because the divine spark burns in our own hearts, and our deepest God-given desires seek to bring it to fulfilment. *We burn with an eternal longing for the infinite.* This is the purpose of our life; this is the goal of all our strivings. This is the driving force through which we laugh and play, make friends, innovate, fall in love, procreate and build empires. The divine spark fires every fibre of our beings, and it illuminates horizons that forever beckon us forth. Around 500 CE, Dionysius the Areopagite expressed it well:

> The divine longing (*theios eros*) is Good seeking good for the sake of the Good ... The divine yearning brings ecstasy so that the lover belongs not to the self but to the beloved ... He is, as it were, beguiled by goodness, by love (*agape*) and by yearning (*eros*) and is enticed away from his eternal dwelling place and comes to abide in all things, and he does so by virtue of his supernatural and ecstatic capacity to remain nevertheless, within himself. (Quoted in McIntosh 1998: 48–9)

These words are reminiscent of what theologians describe as the kenotic outpouring of God in Jesus (cf. Phil. 2:6–7). God emptied that which made God uniquely divine in order to identify with our humanity, thus exalting it to new heights of wholeness and integrity. In the letter to the Philippians, the emptying is described as a precondition for the humiliation and suffering through which Jesus brings about the redemption and exaltation of humanity. This interpretation is congruent with the post-resurrection understanding of Jesus developed in the early Church.

Primordially, we can suggest an alternative reading favoured by feminist scholars (e.g., Mary Grey 2003): namely, that it is the nature of the divine to birth-forth divine life in all creatures, making each and all an expression of the divine, yearning for that fullness of life depicted in John's Gospel. In other words, the fullness of life is facilitated not through suffering and diminution, but through pouring forth in prodigious birthing. As indicated in previous chapters, this notion also features in our understanding of the Great Earth Mother Goddess.

In contemporary jargon, it appears we are hard-wired for divine fulfilment! Not through death and reward in a life to come, but already in our present existence! And not through traditional pain, suffering and the transcendence of all desire (also in Buddhism), but by incorporation into the divine yearning, in which all desiring finds its true home. Desire is not something to get rid of. Instead it is a dimension of experience to be embraced, befriended and transformed in accordance with the divine desire to birth life afresh in every sphere of the divine-cosmic-earthly-creaturely-human creation.

Denuded of our capacity for mystery and the infinite, we atrophy, shrivel and end up turning to all sorts of compensations to feed our deep desires. We create a culture awash with addictions. Desire has been disconnected and in several cases flourishes like a deadly virus. And we won't remedy our plight by taming our drives, but by reclaiming them in their true cosmic and spiritual context. In each new generation we revisit the mystical wisdom, because, as creatures of desire, intuitively we know it is the one enduring resource that will deliver liberating hope and creative possibility.

The mystic in action

A vast literature exists on the subject of mysticism. Christian writers (e.g. Evelyn Underhill 1911; Bernard McGinn 1994; Marc McIntosh 1998) tend to emphasise the transcendent dimension, the ecstatic attachment to God, as the one and only thing that matters. They also highlight the great chasm between the ultra holiness of the divine and the fragility of the human condition.[18] Mysticism tends to be portrayed as the grace bestowed on the selected few, and many of the historical models tend to be those from monasteries and enclosed convents.

No doubt the leading writers would claim that I have distorted their understanding of mysticism. There are indeed several nuances to the interpretation of this subject. What I am portraying above is a popular and widespread understanding which, inappropriately or otherwise, often draws support from the sources I cite.

The dilemma I wish to address here is twofold. Firstly, I believe the Christian tradition particularly has over-spiritualised the mystical experience, and secondly, because of this, we tend to underestimate the earth-bound nature of mystical engagement. I want to suggest that the mystical call is one of transformative engagement at four central levels of life.

1. It involves a perceptual revolution

> The mystic is not detached from history, but committed to it as transformation, starting from a nucleus of transcendent meaning and a minimal utopian dimension which, in as much as it is religious, enables the mystic to be more perceptive than anyone else.
>
> *Leonardo Boff (1995)*

Don Cupitt (1998), Leonardo Boff (1995) and William Johnston (2006) explore this dimension with great insight and clarity. Cupitt suggests that the mystic breaks through the superficiality of all our human constructs, pointing us to alternative ways of knowing, meaning and depth. He goes on to suggest that mysticism may thus be understood as the forerunner to deconstructionist philosophy. What it seeks to undermine more than anything else is the ideological presuppositions of rational thought and patriarchal governance.

In a similar vein, John Jeffrey Kripal (2001: xii) writes:

> One of the defining features of the mystical life is its collapsing of the inside and the outside, a kind of fusion or boundary crossing that recognizes no ultimate differentiation from the rest of the universe, be it naturally or culturally defined. It is a stretching towards excess, transcending all human boundaries, unrelentingly inviting humans to cosmic horizons of desire, suffocated by the dysfunctional world-view we take so much for granted.

2. It transgresses our neat, dualistic divisions, using the psychosexual as a catalyst to release a new revelation of intimacy with the divine

> There is no point at all in blinking the fact that the raptures of the theistic mystic are closely akin to the transports of sexual union.
>
> *R.C. Zaehner (in Kripal 2001)*

Evelyn Underhill (1911) outlines the five stages of mystical development, noted by several commentators: (a) the awakening of the self to the spiritual life; (b) purgation; (c) illumination; (d) the dark night of the soul; (e) union. While most commentators attribute the unitive dimension to a distinctive type of divine rapture, some also note the intense sexual passion that can accompany this experience. It tends to be misinterpreted and dismissed as temptation from Satan, whereas, in fact, it may be precisely the moment when the Holy One is engaging the psyche most deeply.

As a human species we have been through a long history of sexual repression. The transformation of desire requires a rebalancing and retrieval that will not be easy, since it is open to misunderstanding on several fronts. A closer and more discerning study of the great mystics can abet us in this undertaking, as illustrated by scholars such as Jordan (2000), Kripal (2001) and Turner (1995).

3. It describes a passionate encounter with the divine, not in some distant heavenly realm but in the immediacy of creation, apprehended in cosmic and earthly terms

> The spiritual life is the existential task of discovering one's truest self in the context of reality apprehended as a cosmic totality. It is the quest for obtaining an optimal relationship between what one truly is and everything that is.
>
> *Peter Van Ness (1992)*

Here we encounter one of the most drastic displacements of the human capacity for desire. Because of the prevalence of the dualistic world view over at least the past 5,000 years, all the major religions associate sanctity with an adversarial stance towards the created order. I believe this has led to some gross misinterpretations of mysticism in all the great religious traditions.

On closer examination, mystics are precisely the people who were rooted unambiguously in creation and their fascination with the Holy One happens within the enveloping mystery of creation itself. Matthew Fox and the Creation-spirituality movement have been to the fore of this process of retrieval (Fox 1984; 1999), and have been frequently dismissed, and even ridiculed, by those who approach the subject from a more academic perspective.

The transformative power of the mystical calling resides precisely, if not primarily, in the encounter with God in the midst of creation. There is no escapism here. The fulfilment of desire is not postulated on some fulfilled state in the hereafter, but rather in a type of radical immersion, reflecting God's own radical immersion in the cosmos at large. *The mystic seeks to companion the Holy One in the unceasing birthing forth of divine gratuity.* This can result in indescribable ecstasy, sometimes intensely pleasurable but often dark and painful.

4. It matures as a fiercely intense desire for justice and the transformation of all sinful structures

> If you think you are advancing toward unity with God or the absolute and are not growing in love and charity toward your fellow person, you are just deluding yourself.
>
> *Huston Smith (in Horgan 2003)*

Mysticism is about immersion in God's world at the service of God's creativity and liberation. There is a passionate intensity to mystical engagement which often results in human misunderstanding, ridicule and subversion. The mystic is endowed with a transparency to reality through which one can see with great clarity, but this also means one is forever confronting pain, anguish, exploitation, desecration. The mystic knows it all, and basically has no escape route: 'Seeing life against the backdrop of infinity can evoke joy, madness, terror, revulsion, love, gratitude, hilarity – or all the above at once. You may delight in the world's astonishing beauty, or despair at its fragility and insignificance' (Horgan 2003: 216). The psychological and spiritual toll can be weighty indeed.

The mystic struggles internally, discerning how best to respond to the complex picture of reality one encounters in the world. It is the persistent faithfulness to this discernment that equips the mystic to promote and model the work of transformation. The mystic shuns no desire, no matter how lowly or confused; and the mystic sees more clearly than anybody else how to reframe desire in the direction of transformation. This unique wisdom is both the blessing and heartache of the mystical calling.

All of which leaves the mystic with basically one choice: opt in, not out. Co-creating a world for a more just and sustainable way of living becomes the life-long goal. And for all of us called to this quality of presence and ministry, we need frequent reminders that without something of the mystic's zeal and passion, none of us is likely to survive in trying to bring about the right relating that is at the heart of Christian faith and belongs integrally to all the faiths known to humankind.

The desert as presence

In Christian spirituality, the desert is the metaphorical image for mystical achievement. Far away from the allurements and attachments of the 'world', the mystic battles it out with the forces of evil and becomes a holy hero for God! Is this another patriarchal projection, particularly suitable for males moulded in a culture of external achievement?

Westerners have given scant attention to the corresponding metaphor in the monastic and mystical traditions of the Far East. The *forest*, rather than the desert, is the sacred space of the divine seeker.[19] Surrounded by luscious, variegated (and wild) growth, rather than barren arid landscape, the mystic in the forest is lured into the grandeur and elegance of God's creation. Indeed, compared to the surrounding beauty, God at times can seem distant and vague; this is probably what the dark night entails for the Eastern mystic.

On closer examination, of course, the desert is not a metaphor for God's absence but for the intensity of the divine presence. In the West we seem to associate the presence largely if not exclusively with humans, as if the rest of creation did not matter, whereas in the East the cosmic and planetary dimensions are also honoured. Despite its cherished significance in the Western tradition, I suggest we replace the *desert* with the metaphor of the *forest*, thereby honouring desire, not just as a human experience but also as a dimension of all creation. Indeed, it is in its cosmic and planetary context that the transformative power of desire becomes so much more accessible and inspiring.

33

The Desire for Soulful Spirituality

When we encounter the Spirit in the ordinariness of life, desire is leading us into a profound discernment.

In mainline Christian thought, the *soul* describes the aspect of embodied existence that distinctly belongs to God and will outlive the body in eternal life or in eternal damnation. In early Christian times a great deal of debate centred on when and how God inserted the soul into the growing foetus. Today, theologians are reluctant to distinguish soul from body, viewing the soul as co-terminus with the body in its growth and development from the earliest stages of fertilisation and foetal development.

Soul has another significance, deemed to be of much greater age and very much in vogue in the closing decades of the twentieth century. In this case the emphasis is on the body within the soul rather than the soul within the body. *Soulful* describes our various attempts to live with the paradoxes of life in a more enlightened and integrated way, knowing that all our longings and efforts are embraced and nurtured by a deeper cosmic and earthly wisdom.

Transforming spirituality

Conventionally, spirituality and the spiritual life describe our transcendence beyond earthly care and preoccupation, in preparation for life with God in the heavenly realm. It demands that we outgrow our concern with our embodied state and not take too seriously all that concerns the 'worldly' realm down here. Life here is deemed to be a vale of tears, a time for trial and suffering. The real is always beyond. Transcendence is the way to holiness and salvation.

Soulfulness signifies something very different. It seeks the sacred in the ordinary, not in the extraordinary, salvation in the goodness of the now, not in the ultimate triumph of the hereafter. Soulfulness takes incarnation seriously, inviting further commitment to, and engagement with, the transformation God desires for all embodied life from cosmos to person. Transcendence is achieved through immanence; the deeper we reach into creation itself, the more we encounter that which we yearn for transcendentally.

The spiritual praxis inevitably veers in a different direction. Instead of the neat dualistic divisions of what is good and what is bad, soulful engagement is more at home in the in-between, in the liminal space, on the cusp of the paradox, in the 'grey' area where skills for discernment are the primary requisite. Befriending the unfolding process of life, we come to realise that God is not so much a ruler from on high, as a catalyst who forever opens up (reveals) meaning from within creation's epic becoming, and illuminates the great mystery particularly through the paradoxes that often baffle and confuse.

How to be soulful

In the last book of *The Republic*, Plato records the Myth of Er in which he claims that each of us is given a unique *daimon* before we are born, and it becomes for each of us the carrier of our destiny. Daimon does not designate a specific class of divine being, but a peculiar mode of activity for which today we would use words like: genius, guardian, innovator, artist or the Jungian archetype of the trickster. Often confused with the notion of the 'demon', the daimon can embrace and honour chaos and confusion which is often excessively moralised and dismissed as an unwelcome influence of a demonic source. (More in Moore 2004: 16–18.)

The daimon represents the intuitive inner wisdom that defies rationality and often invites us to embrace eccentricity, fragility, vulnerability, contradiction and paradox, as realms of experience that divulge deep meaning, and honour deep desire. At times in life when our spirit feels restless, and conventional cultural expectations feel unreal or even false, the chances are that our daimon-insight may be persuading us that another wisdom is at work which must not be hastily dismissed. This is precisely what contemporary writers mean by the revived notion of *soul* or *soulfulness*.

Thomas Moore (1992; 1994; 2004) is one of the leading theorists on the retrieval of soul. He suggests five characteristics for soulful living:

- *Imagination:* Our conventional culture has indoctrinated us in a cult of literalism that cherishes objectivity and reductionism. The creative mind is stultified and this often crushes the exuberance of the living spirit. Apathy on the one hand and wanton violence on the other are often the ensuing tragedies. We need to honour and release our capacity for the artistic, the poetic, the creative. We need a radically revamped education system and a great deal more trust in mutual exploration.
- *Ordinariness:* We live in a highly competitive world where achievement based on power is exalted and commitment to the ordinary is undervalued and often subverted. Even in the most highly industrialised countries less than 50 per cent of people work in the formal economy. The majority commit their time and talent to more ordinary tasks such as home-making, parenting, voluntary work, artistic pursuits, recreational activities. Without these undertakings our work culture would be oppressive and the overall quality of life would lack lustre and lightness. Commitment to the ordinary is the foundation upon which the extraordinary is made possible.
- *Polytheism:* Most cultures seek monotheistic heroes onto whom we project our hopes and expectations. Frequently this leads to dangerous forms of idolatry, particularly in the religious, political and commercial spheres. Diversity (polytheism) is the basis on which the richness of nature and creation flourishes. Our pre-occupation with heroes leads to power games, separations and exclusions. Creation invites us to work more directly for empowerment, mutuality and inclusiveness.
- *Befriending complexity:* The mechanistic world view, dominant since the sixteenth century, leads to gross simplicity and reduc-tionism. The hidden motivation tends to be power and control. Whatever the practical benefits of this arrangement, it fails dis-mally to honour human desiring which, as indicated in previous chapters, yearns for richness and diversity, congruent with the complexity on which evolution thrives and life flourishes.

- *Embracing paradox:* For the patriarchal culture of divide-and-conquer, we must keep life as logical, rational and manageable as possible. This is a prescription for alienation flying in the face of the untidy, chaotic and paradoxical way in which life flourishes at every level of creation. Even our pathologies and deviations, our vulnerability and fragility, carry important lessons to teach us if we could listen to them attentively instead of the moralistic strategy of trying to suppress and eliminate them as promptly and efficiently as possible.

> To the soul memory is more important than planning, art more compelling than reason, and love more fulfilling than understanding. We know we are well on the way toward soul when we feel attachment to the world and the people around us, and when we live as much from the heart as from the head. We know soul is being cared for when our pleasures feel deeper than usual, when we can let go of the need to be free of complexity and confusion, and when compassion takes the place of distrust and fear. Soul is interested in the differences among cultures and individuals, and within ourselves it wants to be expressed in uniqueness if not in eccentricity.
>
> *Thomas Moore (2004)*

Soul and sexuality

As indicated in previous chapters, an enormous amount of healing needs to be activated in the sexual realm and this can only happen when we begin to liberate our sexuality from the imprisonment of biological reductionism. Peter Black (2003: 119) claims that the task before us is not to keep curbing desire, but rather to keep growing and deepening desire. Our sexual hunger is an ecstatic yearning for the divine, which, when neglected, causes chasms that are quickly filled by addictions. Desire is the hunger of the soul and not merely the fruit of unbridled passion. Desire is born of the erotic Spirit whose breathing forth and birthing forth is the basis of all arousal.

Undoubtedly, desire needs to be channelled and subjected to a healthy discipline (frequently emphasised by Wendy Farley 2005), but, firstly, it needs to be understood, appropriated creatively and rehabilitated in supportive spaces at every level of life: cultural, ethical, interpersonal and personal. This is where soul and sex meet (Moore 1998). We need to revision sexuality in its trans-biological context, as a power for creativity and spirituality. This reconstruction will evoke a very different ethical framing from the narrow moralistic norms that characterise most of the great religions. This may well prove to be the single greatest transformation facing humanity for the foreseeable future.

Soulfulness and transformation

In this time of widespread global change, many people feel a sense of panic and trepidation. In such a culture, we seek certitude, clarity and rationally compelling arguments. We dread complexity and the open-ended nature of reality. And we will tend to follow leaders who promise us a clear way forward; we will even follow them when it is obvious that they are unable to deliver on their utopian promises.

Not much soulfulness in all this, and not much potential for transformation! Desire is reduced to a cerebral set of safe securities. The world of soul and imagination has been shrivelled and perverted. Deep desire is seen to be a dangerous distraction from more pressing concerns. Conformity rather than transformation is the inevitable outcome.

> One of the great conflicts in life is the conflict between ego and soul. The ego is threatened, competitive and stressed, whereas the soul is drawn more towards surprise, spontaneity, the new and the fresh.
>
> *John O'Donohue (1997)*

To negotiate this pilgrim way we need a spirituality big enough to embrace the beckoning horizons, yet grounded enough to accommodate the extraordinary potential of even the most ordinary things. This is the spirituality of soulfulness, capable of holding the enormous potential alongside the paradoxes which baffle and confuse so many in our time. Escape is no longer a useful spiritual strategy; in fact it never was. Ours is a participatory universe, and therein alone can the transformation of desire be duly honoured.

34

Recovering Desire in the Power of Art

To fulfil their creative desires, humans need artists to dream and inspire new ways of seeing.

Already in the 1970s, social theorists such as Fred Polak (1973) claimed that modern art, with the tendency to focus on the emptiness and shallowness of the here-and-now, had seriously betrayed its role as a catalyst for cultural and personal transformation. As art forms – art, music, literature – became absorbed in the lurid, the banal and the obscene, often portraying the human as a robot made up of lifeless lines, surfaces, angles and spheres, the artist seems to be indulging in an exercise of nihilistic self-absorption.

Committed to portraying reality as it is, the artist is in danger of betraying the challenge to inspire and proffer hope in a desired future. Symbolism is abandoned in favour of reductionistic literalism. Art seems increasingly incapable of serving the desires of the human soul.

In more recent times, a contemporary British artist, Alan Manktelow, suggests (2005: 21) that the artist is still stuck in the nihilistic spiral: 'The art of our times seems to sink ever deeper into a quagmire of incomprehensibility and the expression of every conceivable kind of negative emotion.' Therefore, it can no longer serve to channel and transform our emotional needs; deprived of this facility, our desires are depraved and our psychic well-being is jeopardised.

Image and the inner soul

Perhaps the crucial issue here is the imaginal realm and its central role in the evolution of human meaning. Carl Jung believed that *soul* and *image* are one and the same and that they exist as a mediating factor between body and mind. The French scholar Henri Corbin (1972; 1998) developed the concept of the *mundus imaginalis* (the imaginal realm), which he describes as a vast intermediate sphere of image and representation that is just as ontologically real as the worlds of sense and intellect. In the domain of the imagination things are *real*, not in the sense that they are being 'imagined' by someone, but are images that have some kind of integrity and existence of their own. The imagination is a phenomenon to be evaluated in its own right (also Casey 2000: 32).

Corbin describes images as the thoughts of the heart, understanding heart as the seat of the imagination. In this sense, images are not something that a person sees – they are not necessarily visual – but rather a perspective, the way one sees, comprehends and understands reality. All of which only makes sense when we adopt a different understanding of the imagination and its role in human living.

Most importantly, we need to distinguish imagination from mind (see Casey 2000). The psychologist James Hillman consistently claims that the mind is in the imagination rather than the imagination in the mind. Imagination belongs not just to the head but to the entire body, and in human terms it is grounded in the human body as it functions interactively with the creative energy of the universe. While we continue to define imagination as a mere processor of perceptions or, worse, as a sphere for daydreaming and wild fantasy, we subvert its more central role as the domain in which we appropriate, channel and process images in our desire to connect creatively with the rest of creation. In the words of Carol Frenier (2005: 13): 'We inhabit the image in order to grow from it.'

All the scholars cited thus far acknowledge the transcendent and archetypal dimension of imagination, and readily connect psychic processes with spiritual aspirations. Imagination of its very nature is transparent to spirit-power. Hillman suggests that the value found in images is in regard to how they present the 'gods' to us, not so much as concrete appearances but rather in what the deities represent for us as metaphors constructed by the human imagination. Imagination at all times is in pursuit of meaning, of viable connection and life-giving relationship. What the divine desires, is ultimately what the imagination is seeking.

Imaging in a literalist world

> Just as imagination is a sign of the soul at work, so worry is a sign of the ego doing everything it can, especially through rational understanding and control, to keep soul locked away.
>
> *Thomas Moore (1994)*

Imagination, and the nourishment made possible through imagining, struggles for integration in a world so addicted to the rational and the literal. Here we encounter a major obstacle to the work of transformation, particularly in the realm of human desiring. Our desires cannot be curtailed by the rational, the quantifiable, the measured, by that which can be subjected to conscious control. Imagination needs the freedom to flow in and out of the mystery within which life is embraced. Imagination needs to be continually stretched and expanded; otherwise it atrophies into delusions and nightmares, the basis for all sorts of addictions and dysfunctionalities. Madness, strictly speaking, is not about mind out of control, but rather the result of a crushed and petrified imagination.

To cultivate and nourish the imagining of the imagination, we need the arts, those dimensions of culture where creativity is allowed to be creative, where fantasy is channelled. When we rehabilitate the aesthetic, spirit-power awakens us to the transcendent in our midst. Without this facility, not alone are we deprived of something important, the very soul of our humanity is robbed, and authentic human living is well nigh impossible.

Evolution thrives on wild creativity. It is full of surprises. In the grand story of cosmic unfolding, things often reach frightening levels of disintegration, as in the great extinctions. Annihilation seems to be the only resolution, but total annihilation is never registered, because this wild creative Spirit swings the pendulum as novel breakthroughs herald a new wave of vitality and future possibility. It makes no rational or logical sense, and I suspect it never will. This is paradox writ large; it makes sense to the creative imagination, and without imagination it spells ruination, despair and nihilism.

The proactive artist

In their desire to be in solidarity with the precarious conditions of our times, artists and writers seek to mirror the gruesome and ugly face of reality for what it is in itself. Objective truth is portrayed as objectively as possible, and it is left to the viewer to do with it whatever he or she wants. Both artist and viewer ignore a basic element of the human condition: *we are not primed for objectivity!* Being creatures of imagination, we are transparent to that which always exceeds the rational and objective.

> Art is the normal development of the soul, the normal means of anamnesis and orientation. Lacking this environment, we starve in the midst of quantitative plenty.
>
> *Kathleen Raine (1991)*

In cultural and systemic terms, the role of the artist is that of a catalyst, the one who prods and provokes, imagines and dreams, conjures up what might be, and could be. The artist is called to be the great generator of hope and not the contemporary pessimist who often plummets us into anomie and despair.

From this perspective, the artist becomes a moral agent, a cultural critic, a justice-awakener – as illustrated by Jan Phillips (2006) in her inspiring work on original thinking. Far from being value-neutral, and therefore only marginally influential, the artist serves as a proactive agent for imaginative possibilities. Indeed, the artist must help us in our time to confront the numbness of death and make transparent all that is being undermined by denial and by fidelity to what is unreal. But the artist must not betray creation's great wisdom in which death is always at the service of rebirth. Nihilism is neither a cosmic nor planetary option.

If the artist succumbs to the nihilistic morbidity s(he) is merely nourishing the cultural addictions of false power and pleasure in which already millions of people are trapped. Caught in the web of this destructive energy, people become more and more reactive. Corrupted desire (rather than *false* desire) takes over. Creative energy is sapped away trying to fill an infernal chasm.

> First, art forms madness rather than represses it. Second, the arts often act as the sensitive antennae of social justice and moral outrage, keeping the soul awake to hypocrisy, cant, suppression and jingoism. And third, the fundamental enemy of all art is mediocrity.
>
> *James Hillman (2004a)*

In the face of such myopic reaction, the artist must remain pro-active! The artist must hold on to the prophetic space that never totally abandons hope (cf. Brueggemann 1978; 1986). Confronting us with the call to conversion, the artist must also point us to what the Christian faith calls *resurrection*. This is the horizon that defies ultimate despair. It may not make much sense to the rational world, but for those who seek to honour the deep desires of the human heart, and recreate possibilities for the transformation of those desires, it is the great non-negotiable. And the artist holds the awe-some responsibility for ensuring its legitimate place in the unfolding fortunes of time and culture.

In this transformative undertaking, the artist and the justice-maker become important collaborators. Indeed, the one can scarcely survive without the other. While the justice-maker seeks the trans-formation of structures and institutions – congruent with authentic desire – the artist provides the vision and inspiration that animates and sustains that effort. That artist provides the beauty that gives transcendent meaning to the call to duty. Together, the artist and the justice-maker recreate hope, and new possibilities for desiring hearts to be made whole once more.

Having reviewed the challenge of the artist, we will now explore the vocation of the justice-maker!

35

Desire Embracing Justice for Liberation

Honouring desire involves not merely internal psychic re-structuring, but also developing social and political structures that promote justice as a key value.

> And although the first birth is of the person, any pedagogy which stops at the Birthing of oneself is simply too narrow for our time. Birthing must spill over to the Birthing of just environments in society itself, for Birth and Breakthrough are 'resurrections into justice.'
>
> *Maria Harris (1997)*

By personalising desire, and over-identifying its power with sexual yearning, we have missed many of its global and earthly challenges. Desire belongs first and foremost to the creative Spirit energising and birthing forth the possibilities of cosmic creativity. These trans-late into earthly presence in the rhythms and movements that beget pattern and process in the earth's unfolding over 4.5 billion years. Desire has a large context which we ignore to our human peril.

This perilous omission hits us in stark relief today as trans-national, marketing forces violate, colonise and exploit human desire to a degree previously unknown. Our capacity for desire has been sequestered to seek out so many things we don't really need, but the colonising world of commercialism has successfully convinced us that we must have them. Instead of seeking to satisfy desire through the inherited satisfactions of cosmic creation, we have been indoctrinated to seek fulfilment through insatiable hungers that create deeper alienation and add to the meaningless suffering in our world.

Justice: a troubled history

Realigning desire with *justice-making* is one strategy to alert us to what is really happening and to encourage us to redress the imbalance. Unfortunately, recent history is not on our side here. To many people justice is a vague, illusive and confusing word. And it has become over-associated with criminal procedures and the procurement of human rights.

Long before the ancient Greeks laid the foundations of jurisprudence (from which both religionists and politicians develop theories of justice),[20] humans realised that we must learn to live in a convivial way with the earth as an organism; otherwise, damage ensues both for us and for the earth we inhabit (see Primavesi 2003; 2004). Our engagement with the earth and our use of its resources must be pursued with care, sustainability and accountability. Humans seem to have managed this interaction with a considerable degree of success, and in the process fulfilled authentic human need. The organised management of agriculture, some 10,000 years ago, is one stage where this otherwise convivial relationship began to break down quite seriously.

Ever since then, human control and domination took precedence, and various spiritualities of mastering and governing the unruly creation were invoked. The rights of humans became a major preoccupation in the theories of justice first developed in classical Greek culture about 2,500 years ago. It is also worthy of note that the interest in justice belonged almost exclusively to the elite in society of the time, and all the guidelines were drawn up with the rich and powerful primarily in mind. Sadly, little seems to have changed in the intervening period.

At the present time, the philosopher John Rawls (1999) is widely considered to be the leading theorist in this field. His theory is based squarely on the assumption that it is natural and innate for people to compete for the goods and resources of the earth: 'that the function of ethical theory is not to reduce this competitive adversarial stance, and replace it with mutual care and community, but simply to provide a framework which would ensure that, given human greed, the distribution of the goods takes place as fairly as possible' (Forrester 1997: 136).

Justice has been collapsed into *fairness*, assuming humans to be in charge of creation, and the right to compete, a God-given endowment. The consumptive desires of the powerful will be met (as if those were the really important desires) and those of the weak don't seem to matter. Amazingly, governments in several contemporary nations, and trans-national corporations, with a modicum of ethical accountability, draw heavily on Rawls' theory.

Justice as love of life

Religions tend to prize charity above justice. In large measure this has resulted from the dualism of the sacred versus the secular, whereby both Church and State have colluded in keeping charity within religion and 'justice' within the secular sphere. Any attempt to reclaim a form of justice that will honour human desiring firstly has to break through this archaic splitting. In so far as religions explore the issue of justice, until recent times the focus was almost entirely on humanly related issues.

> We show little or no understanding of love when we make charity the counterpart and supplement of, or substitute for, justice. Love is co-extensive with justice ... justice is the efficacious, institutional and social realisation of love.
>
> *Paul Ricoeur (1964)*

Substitute desire for love in the quote from Ricoeur above, and we captivate the essence of justice in its deepest meaning, where it becomes an essential dimension for the transformation being explored in this book. Essentially, *justice deals with the procedures and structures that facilitate life-giving relationships for all, as well as for the earth we inhabit and the cosmos to which we belong.* This requires that we begin to outgrow the tribalistic, nationalistic and ethnic entities we have invented so that we can reclaim more generic ways of regional cooperation, ways that honour the complexity and diversity of the creation we inhabit.

There is a mode of relating that befits the earth and its organic processes, and adopting that relationality is essentially what justice-making is about. If we wish to live from a place of hope, rather than from within the despair and nihilism which is beginning to dominate our world, we need to move urgently into a more just way of living and behaving.

Justice and globalisation

In our globalised world of trans-national corporations, striving to live justly can be a daunting task. So much exploitation takes place, in the face of which we often feel helpless and even hopeless. And growing numbers realise that governments themselves collude with the trans-national forces. Governments also adopt violent strategies to accrue harmony and peace among warring nations and factions. Millions have already lost faith in political systems; nor do they see much inspiration coming from the religions. The rhetoric about justice-making can begin to feel scary and depressing.

I wish to submit that the God who imbued creation with the desire for better times ahead – the God who always fulfils the promise (see Haught 1993) – never intended humans to live with such despair and anomie. With utter defiance we must not capitulate to such an erosion of desire, the very antithesis of the transformation I explore in these pages. Two strategies can begin to orient us in the direction of hope and promise.

Firstly, as indicated in previous chapters, all intentionality belongs primarily to creation, and the power of intention underpins all action and all physical form. Action follows thought. If enough people begin to think differently, and imagine more laterally, in time we can co-create the conditions that augment transformative change. We need to be very vigilant around the quality of our thinking, even in small things, and we need to ensure that we regularly feed the mind with constructive and creative ideas. In that way we can contribute to building up the new envelope of consciousness. A regular meditation practice is crucial to this endeavour (see note 1).

> It often happens that we have knowledge of what oppresses us but we do not have the means to change the rules of the game of oppression. Knowledge is certainly important in this process of transformation, but it is not enough to bring about actual change.
>
> *Ivone Gebara (2002)*

Secondly, networking is likely to be an essential organisational survival skill for the future. As major institutions break down and can no longer embrace the deep desires of the human heart, networks are likely to emerge as the creative alternative. So, too, for justice-making. Beyond the paltry efforts of governments to engage the major issues of our time, a great deal more is being achieved by creative networks like Greenpeace, Friends of the Earth, International Forum for Globalisation and many more. These associations, built around the principles of power from the base up, name and engage the crucial issues of our time with a clarity and comprehensiveness that put most governments to shame. Over the past twenty years, any gestures made by governments to address current ecological problems have tended to be the result of instigation from networks like Greenpeace. The real power for transformation is with networks and not with major governments.

None of us on our own can confront the major justice questions of our time. The experience will overwhelm and depress us. However, we can exert power and influence by joining networks and giving them our personal and practical support. This may be much more hope-filled and empowering than engaging in formal political activity.

Beyond the human

Transformative desire includes the human person while also transcending the human sphere. The justice that honours that which is deepest in our hearts, must also be the justice that protects and enhances the growth and evolution of creation. Justice-making to enhance the human has to be geo-justice or eco-justice. People can only know real justice when the justice-strategies are so designed as to maximise the benefits for creation. Otherwise, the earth's needs are neglected and human desiring is once more impoverished.

This requires us to reframe our concern with *human rights*. The basic rights of shelter, clothing, food, health care, education, employment, freedom from oppression, etc., are all dependent on a healthy wholesome earth. Thomas Berry (in Dreyer and Burrows 2005: 244) advocates that all organisms including planet earth itself acknowledge three foundational rights: *(a) the right to be; (b) the right to habitat; (c) the right to fulfil its role in the great community of existence* (more in Cullinan 2003). Consequently, *rights* are meaningless without the corresponding notion of *duties*. In fact, it is more accurate to claim that we only have duties (i.e., responsibilities) and when these are all fulfilled authentically, then our rights are safeguarded.

The hedonistic, consumerist culture of our time is grossly preoccupied with rights. Egotistical demands often transcend all other considerations. This is anthropocentrism gone wild, like a cancerous growth addicted to its own perpetuation. One aspect, staunchly defended by some religions in the past, is the notion of private property. This is an aberration of the cosmic will-to-belong. In the words of the Jewish mystic Elliot Wolfson (quoted in Kripal 2001: 269): 'Belonging, therefore, is the very opposite of possessing; it involves being possessed.' Belonging is about sharing and mutual responsibility, not about private ownership and hoarding.

Justice and sustainability

> Take only your share; Clean up after you;
> Leave the home in good repair for future occupants.
>
> *Sallie McFague (2001)*

A greater integration of rights and duties orients us towards living in a more sustainable way. We become more aware of the need to live in harmony with all other creatures with whom we share the planet; in meeting their desires in a more integrated way we advance our own dignity and worth. Theologian Carol Christ (1997: 167) delineates nine touchstones to guide us on our way:

> Nurture life.
> Walk in love and beauty.
> Trust the knowledge that comes through the body.
> Speak the truth about conflict, pain and suffering.
> Take only what you need.
> Think about the consequences of your actions.
> Approach the taking of life with great restraint.
> Practice great generosity.
> Repair the web.

My desires will be justly accommodated when all other desires can be authentically honoured. And this cannot be achieved without prior consideration for the creation that birthed us all and to which we all primordially belong. When that context is upheld, and not compromised, then the transformation of desire can be attained. Justice will reign; peace will ensue, and creation can become what evolution desires it to be.

36

Desire and the New Reign of God

Jesus took desire seriously and wishes all Christians to do the same. To make desire transformative in daily life, Jesus offered a radically new vision which Christian churches struggle to integrate.

The early Christians channelled their desires through the cultural constructs of their day. Messianic figures proliferated in that culture; Jesus was one among many. For the people of the time, the *king* was considered to be the primary mediator of divine power in the world. Consequently, all those with messianic aspirations could only be authentic if they had sprung from kingly origins or somehow were linked with royal patronage. Connection with kingship was the seal of messianic authenticity.

The story we have inherited as a Christian people belongs to this cultural landscape. On the basis of this story we have penned our hopes and sought the fulfilment of our deepest desires. But the transformative effect of that story varies enormously through the ages, and even the original context is differently understood as new research brings other dimensions to light.

Millennial desires

The world that Jesus entered was seething with human longings that showed in messianic dreams, millennial fantasies, apocalyptic desperation, mystical revelations, suicidal nationalism, religious critique and reform, reactionary rigidity, and a sense that time was collapsing, that the future was foreshortened, that the mystery of reality was about to be revealed. In such a milieu, the authenticity of Jesus was like a beacon that drew all mythological beliefs to itself. Incubating in the womb of that period was God's rash gamble that humanity might become more humane.

Walter Wink (2002)

I suggest it was not a rash gamble from God's point of view. Humanity had come through an evolutionary trajectory of some 6,000,000 years, and the *incarnational* God had accompanied us throughout that entire process. For the greater part, the evolutionary gamble had paid dividends; for most of the time humans had co-operated with the evolving process of life, and now were reaching a high point of evolutionary development. At that axial moment, God in Jesus – and in the great incarnational figures of the other religions – affirms and confirms the human project. God saw that it was good – and for Christians, Jesus is the earthly manifestation (revelation) of that statement.

In terms of our great human story, Jesus embodies both the apex of human achievement and the forerunner of humanity's next evolutionary leap.[21] The resurrected Jesus symbolises what humans can yet become, the transformation we must continually undergo if desire is to be appropriately fulfilled.

Symbolically Jesus does represent a 'new reign', but with little resemblance to the old regime of earthly kingship. That was the great mistake of the early Christ followers, and it continues to haunt Christians to our own time.

The Kingdom of God

Jesus spoke frequently of a new kingdom taking shape under his instigation and serving as the inspiration for his words and deeds. The Gospels refer to it as the *Kingdom of God*, often described as the *New Reign of God* in current scholarship. It has nothing to do with earthly kingship. In fact, it is the antithesis of royal power as understood then and now. Jesus seems to have invoked royal language and imagery as a subversive strategy for the breakthrough he was seeking to activate (see Herzog 1994; 2004). Appropriating the kingly context of his life and times, he kept turning it on its head, declaring it moribund, while inaugurating a new 'reign' in which empowerment rather than power would be the central feature.

Most of the early Christians, particularly the twelve apostles, failed to grasp the message. It was too original, provocative and prophetic for their conditioned minds. They had been heavily indoctrinated by the reductionistic culture of patriarchy. The horizon of their desiring was hidebound by the cult of earthly kingship and they could not envisage transformation except within that earthly context: the messianic liberator would have to be king-like! And what a massive disappointment he proved to be when he did not fulfil their limited expectations.

Two thousand years later, it would appear that little has changed. Exalted christologies still flourish, and the transformed vision of a new heaven and a new earth inaugurated by Jesus has yet to be realised. And the human species, still struggling to find its way through the patriarchal maze, has not really taken Jesus seriously. Had we done so, desiring and its transformative power would be differently understood. Walter Wink (2002: 256) summarises our dilemma:

> As bearer of the archetype of the Human Being, Jesus activates the numinous power that is capable of healing, transforming, or rebirthing those who surrender themselves to it. As such, Jesus knew himself to be in the grip of a power greater than he. A problem arises at just this point, however. When Jesus is worshipped as the sole bearer of the archetype of humanness, He is made a supernatural being. As such he loses his connection to the struggle to be human, and becomes a cult figure in a religion focussed on his person (individual) rather than on the reality he bore.

The crisis facing the Christian churches in our times has little to do with the popular diagnosis of ageing congregations and diminishing clergy, with moral issues or ethical behaviours. The churches are in crisis because they are failing to honour the radical, prophetic dream of their founder. Consequently, legitimate human desire is not being fulfilled, and the transformation which ecclesial communities claim to provide cannot be mediated authentically. People drift away because authentic desire is not being nourished.

Nor can the contemporary churches provide a cultural counter-witness to the colonising and subjugation of desire by the consumerist forces of our time. The churches themselves, in many cases, have been co-opted into the consumer culture. They even try to market spirituality as a useful commodity to woo the confidence and loyalty of a confused public (see Carrette and King 2005).

Healing and empowerment

Scripture scholar John Dominic Crossan (1991; 1994) claims that *healing* and *commensality* are the key features of the new vision of Jesus encapsulated in the rubric of the Kingdom of God. Commensality refers to the open, shared table from which Jesus never excluded anybody, the table at which the rejects (prostitutes, tax collectors and sinners) held equal place with those considered to be of good repute. Commensality denotes *empowerment* – a quality of affirmation and inclusiveness whereby people could begin to reclaim self-worth and dignity – because their basic desires were being honoured and augmented.

Healing in this context is not about miraculous cures. As Davies (1995) indicates, the healing ministry of Jesus probably involved encounters wherein Jesus as a Spirit-possessed healer invoked altered states of consciousness to realign the damaged spirit-infused energy of the other, thus restoring the psychic balance that led to wholeness and well-being. Here we witness the transformation of desire in very clear relief, which indeed might have been the catalyst that enabled people to leave all and follow Jesus (as Davies intimates); many of the disciples were probably people who had been healed by Jesus.

The healing and empowerment, however, is not confined to people. Systems are also the target of this transformation. People belong to systems, structures and institutions, all of which affect and influence us far more profoundly than most of us realise. The liberation Jesus proclaimed and activated was first and foremost a freedom from political oppression and stultifying religiosity, from the material and economic binds of those who usurped indigenous resources to their own benefit (mainly the Romans), and those who perpetuated a cult of purity accompanied by legal details almost impossible to fulfil (mainly the Jews).

Two thousand years later, the clarion Gospel call 'set my people free' still echoes around the Christian world with a frightening shallowness. Where freedom has been implemented in the name of Christian faith it always has strings attached, many of which have been imperialistic and colonial. Within the body of the Christian churches themselves, women still battle for equality and justice. Christianity still clings to a past, embedded in Roman power and Greek rationalism. For much of the reign of Christendom, the counter-cultural empowerment of the Kingdom has not been taken seriously and, in many situations, has been disturbingly subverted.

Kingdom transformation

As in the other major religions, desire is problematic in Christian faith-practice. The word is strongly associated with greed, lust and egoism. All desire is precarious and ultimately dangerous. It is something to get rid of, not to embrace. Transformation of desire in Christian life effectively means elimination of desire.

In this analysis religion breaks loose from the chain of life. It becomes an instrument of death and destruction. It undermines that which is central to all spiritual growth and development. The desires of the heart are precisely those that keep us rooted in mystery, forever reminding us that the Spirit lures us forth into the transformative power of the new. This is precisely what is happening in every one of the parable stories in the Gospels, the seminal narratives offered by Jesus to break open the meaning of the Kingdom of God.

Jesus took desire seriously, and wishes all Christians to do the same. We engage desire, not primarily by adopting a moralistic and legal coding, but by working co-operatively for the right relationships that facilitate liberation and growth at every level of life. *Striving to get relationships right is the heart and soul of the New Reign of God.* And it is not merely human relationships, but right relating at every level from the cosmos to the bacterial realm. Creation is forever held in the embrace of a relational matrix, and from that foundational source all relationships find their true place and purpose.

Conclusion to Part Three

The Restless Heart Brings Enduring Peace!

The restlessness of the human heart is a divine endowment. Born from mystery we are programmed for mystery. It could not be otherwise in a creation which itself flourishes on mystery. The restlessness comprises the pain and ecstasy of every act of birth. Birthing forth new possibility, involving the dark night of disillusionment and death, is our life's work.

The mystery, therefore, for which we are programmed is our co-creative responsibility for birthing the new. This is the primordial base for all our desires. Every urge of the flesh, every stroke of the artist's pen, all the great inventions of humankind, along with our unconscious drive for dominance and control, are born from this primal longing. Our yearnings are deep and ancient, as old as the great Spirit who has inspired creation throughout aeons, and whom we can only glimpse in a dim and distant way.

As creatures of cosmic mystery and earthy grounding, we are blessed with resources far beyond our imaginings. These resources become precarious, even to the point of being demonic, when they are not utilised creatively. This is where the transformation of desire is tried and tested. This is where the sheer power of goodness is often undermined and perverted.

All our resources are for the task of birthing forth the new. At every juncture in the inspiring work of the creative Spirit, opportunities open up for the desires of the human heart. God's Spirit and our spirit are in fundamental alignment, and evolution's story confirms that fact several times over. But when we forget our true story, then, indeed, it is difficult, in fact impossible, to honour what we are really meant to be about.

So, the task of transformation may be summarised in a synthesis I borrow from the Scripture scholar Walter Brueggemann (1993: 55ff.). We face a triple conversion out of amnesia, greed and despair and a triple challenge to re-member, relate and hope:

- *Being a people who have largely forgotten our true story (amnesia), we end up with a dis-membered understanding of life; we need to re-member what we have so brutally fragmented.*
- *In our brutalised world, with desire as the greatest casualty, inordinate fear drives our selfish greed and self-aggrandisement; we need to reclaim our place in the relational web of life and re-learn how to relate creatively and responsibly.*
- *From a dominant culture of confusion and fear, we often live on the verge of personal and collective despair. On the other hand, cosmic and planetary creation thrives on hope, a hope that always sees the promise of life fulfilled, a promise which also embraces humankind, a promise which we must learn to embrace once more – with vigour and enthusiasm!*

Notes

1. In many of the great spiritual traditions, *meditation* is the primary means to cultivate and nurture a life of *contemplation*. It includes a vast range of practical exercises, associated with breathing, mental concentration and restfulness, as means of disposing the human spirit to be more receptive to the divine spirit. Meditation carries far more significance in the great Eastern religious traditions than in the West, in which formal prayer and penance were considered more congruent with the contemplative life. In other words, prayer was about banishing human desire rather than integrating it.

   In the closing decades of the twentieth century, meditation became a new spiritual fashion for millions around the world. A new search for interiority seems to have been let loose. Eastern forms, e.g., Transcendental Meditation, were widely adopted, while Western versions, e.g., the Jesus Prayer (cf. www.WCCM.org), Centering Prayer (www.thecentering.org/ centering_method.html), gained extensive popularity. More cerebral approaches to prayer and worship lost appeal while millions began to explore – and still do – spiritual meaning using many different techniques, but notably those which favour stillness and silence.

   In several contemporary approaches to meditation, the distinction between the sacred and the secular dissolves (www.en.wikipedia.org/wiki/niki/meditation). Agnostics, even atheists, practise meditation with the same commitment and regularity as religious believers. The great mystery within which all life is held evokes a search for meaning and inner peace in all humans, irrespective of religious affiliation. (Several valuable insights in William Johnston's autobiography (2006).)

2. Human origins is a hotly debated issue right now. Contemporary palaeontologists distinguish between the genus *Australopithecus*, which describes the Great Ape lineage of gorillas, chimpanzees, bonobos and hominids, deemed to be more ape-like than human, and the genus *Homo*, for the human lineage from Homo Habilis of some 2.5 million years ago down to humans alive today. However, this distinction is no longer considered to be watertight as we establish more and more human-like features in ancestors going right back to some 6,000,000 years ago, the temporary date for our most recently discovered ancestor, Toumai Man, excavated in Chad, North Africa in July 2001 by the French palaeontologist Michel

Brunet (see *Nature*, Vol. 434, 7 April 2005, 752–5). Several valuable web pages illustrate the exciting debate on human origins, from which I recommend the following: www.cradleofhumankind.co.za and www.becominghuman.org

3. Throughout the book I use the terms 'patriarchy' and 'patriarchal' to describe forms of governance and control in which power from on high is hierarchically mediated from the top to the base – prioritising the rational, cerebral mode of understanding. Men have been largely conditioned to exercise this approach, and until recent decades, women – and children – were totally excluded.

   I date the rise of the patriarchal value-system to about 10,000 years ago to coincide with the shadow side of the Agricultural Revolution. I do not dispute the positive values of the Agricultural Revolution, but many contemporary scholars are reluctant to acknowledge the downside of that same development: the violence, exploitation, power-seeking, objectifying the land, displacing thousands of indigenous species, and letting loose diseases never known previously to humankind. (More in Eisenberg 1998; Manning 2004.)

4. Academic textbooks often use phrases like 'the dawn of civilization', the rise of civilisation', 'the beginnings of civilisation'. Civilisation tends to be defined in terms of (a) the development of writing in the Sumerian culture of the Tigris-Euphrates valley about 6,000 years ago, and (b) the emergence of the first cities in the Eastern Mediterranean world around the same time. Having checked several sources, I am still not clear why these two criteria have been selected for our definition of civilisation. What I find particularly disturbing is the implication that back beyond the time frame of 6,000 years everything was uncivilised, primitive and barbaric. Here one detects echoes of the arrogance, anthropocentrism and shortsightedness that often seems to characterise patriarchal forms of governance. It can beget a dangerously reductionistic view of reality.

5. Archetypal psychologist James Hillman (2004b) claims that the violence of warfare arises from an archetypal impulse, a timeless force, a paradoxical allurement as old as humanity itself. There are several similarities with the views of René Girard, and similar underlying flaws in the argument. All his evidence is based on male sources, largely from within the past few millennia; the failure to surface female sources undermines his claim to archetypal universality. Much more fruitful lines of enquiry are adopted by Erich Fromm (*The Anatomy of Human Destructiveness*, New York: Henry Holt and Co., 1973) who argues that sadistic violence is rooted in the attempt to turn impotence into omnipotence, to exercise total control, and by William Cavanaugh (1998) who expounds the notion of torture as a ritualization of omnipotence.

6. This socio-economic theory was first developed by a Scottish engineer, Major C.H. Douglas, after the First World War. It is often described as The Basic Citizen's Income, the Social Dividend or Social Credit. It has

been extensively studied by economists and is known to be economically viable. It is political, cultural and classicist resistance that makes it unworkable. For more information, see www.douglassocialcredit.com/html/social_credit.html

7. Christian faith suggests that the Holy Spirit was first bestowed at Pentecost, shortly after the death of Jesus – and bestowed only on *humans*. In the Christian sacramental system, the Holy Spirit is initially conferred at baptism. For some years now, Christian theologians have tried to expand the role and understanding of the Holy Spirit, right up to the seminal works of Denis Edwards (2004) and Mark I. Wallace (2005), both of whom suggest the Spirit's full involvement in the cosmic creation since the beginning of creation.

8. Ever since the publication of Dan Brown's *The Da Vinci Code* (2003), the concept of the Great Mother Goddess has been given a new lease of life – although very poorly explained in the book. This subject has evoked intense debate and reflection particularly among feminists, throughout the closing decades of the twentieth century. For an excellent résumé, see *Feminist Theology*, 13 (Jan. 2005). Ruether (2005) also provides a comprehensive overview and a valuable critique.

9. Frequently, scholars link the tradition of the Mother Goddess with the notion of the Black Madonna in the Christian tradition, a depiction of Mary known across much of the Christian world. More in Barham 2003; Begg 1996; Gebara and Bingemer 1989.

10. India seems to hold the record for the highest rate of suicide among farmers, sometimes due to inclement weather, but more often due to exploitation of the land for Western corporate interests. Several web pages also describe an increase in farmers' suicides in Europe, USA, Canada and Brazil. See www.commondreams.org/views03/0912-01.htm

11. George Coyne, former Director of the Vatican Observatory, makes an important observation, namely that as well as the dynamics of chance and necessity, cosmic evolution is characterised by *fertility*, and it is this third feature in particular that gives evolution a sense of purpose and direction ('Infinite wonder of the divine', *The Tablet*, 10 Dec. 2005, 6–7). It is unfortunate that Pope Benedict XVI in his first encyclical, *Deus Caritas Est*, tends to equate the erotic with Greek fertility cults, which in turn he makes synonymous with temple prostitution. This oversimplifies and misjudges a much more complex phenomenon, and could distract from the deeper analysis which the subject material deserves.

12. The Internet offers several interesting and encouraging examples of bioregional-type initiatives, e.g., www.en.wikipedia.org/wiki/bioregionaldemocracy and www.greatriv.org/bioreg.htm

13. In the 1970s, Raymond Dasmann, wildlife ecologist, in collaboration with Peter Berg, then Director of the Plant Drum Foundation in California USA, helped to redraw the global map in terms of its biotic provinces for the purposes of the conservation of plants and animals. A distinction

began to emerge between ecosystem people who for millennia lived within, and were dependent on, the local ecosystems for survival, and modern biospheric people who exploit the entire globe for trade in products, breaking down watershed and ecosystem constraints (more in www.planetdrum.org).

Alexander (1990) claims that bioregionalism is an ideal rather than something existing on the ground. He provides a useful overview of the leading theories while noting the formidable challenge of translating those theories into workable programmes. What he fails to identify is the addictive lure of the prevailing socio-economic order which effectively requires humans to relate with the earth as a commodity that can be purchased, used and exploited by the highest bidder.

14. At a later stage, I will explore possible links with divine meaning. For now, I want to honour the wisdom so elegantly exhibited in the workings of the body itself. To invoke a divine explanation too quickly runs a distinctive danger not of explaining how things work, but rather of explaining them away.

15. Scholars tend to regard the *chimpanzee* as the primate which most closely resembles the human, sharing 98.4 per cent of the same DNA. However, since the middle of the twentieth century there has been another contender, namely the *bonobo*, found thus far only in the Republic of the Congo. This is a very different creature from the chimpanzee, far less violent and highly co-operative, far more congruent with the dynamic of desire I explore in this book. For more on the bonobos and possible links with humans, see Frans de Waal (1997; 2005); web page: www.en.wikipedia.org/wiki/Bonobo

16. For much of the twentieth century, just when rationality seems to have reached an unassailable monopoly, the role of intuition and imagination came under intense investigation. This alternative perspective on how we view reality is often referred to as the *imaginal*; further information in Corbin (1972; 1998); Hillman (1992; 2004a). Of related interest is Jan Phillips' (2006) seminal work on original thinking.

17. *Adult Education* requires a very different focus and strategy from that of young people: see web page www.adulted.about.com/cs/learningtheory/ For an extensive bibliography, see www.infed.org/lifelonglearning/b-aeprin.htm

18. At times this can lead to the disturbing sense of having lost one's faith, a haunting agnosticism that may last for years. Writers old and modern allude to this phenomenon. See Cupitt (1998); Horgan (2003); Johnston (2006).

19. There are several web pages on Forest Monks in the Buddhist tradition spread throughout several Asian countries. The following written sources are insightful on the *forest* as a spiritual metaphor: Satavayu, 'The Forest Way', *The Turning Wheel: Journal of Socially Engaged Buddhism* (Winter 2002–2003), 33–4; 'Going Forth – the Call of the Forest', *Dharma Life*, Issue 16 (Summer 2001)*.

20. From the Greeks we have inherited a somewhat confused depiction of justice. Socrates tried to work with three fundamental principles: that there is such a thing as justice; that it is not easy to know what justice is; and that knowing and doing justice requires a quality of asceticism if we are to overcome the obstacles that get in the way. Plato, adopting these principles, considered justice to be objectively real and essential to constrain and channel the use of power, primarily through the constitution of an ideal state. (More in Forrester 1997: 43ff.)

Such aspirations sound very noble until we note that, for both Socrates and Plato, the dialogue on what constitutes justice and how it should be implemented was for elite males only, with slaves, workers and women having no say whatever. In truth, this conception of justice is largely about the deployment of power and social status. And it is exclusively about human beings and their rights; other species and the earth itself are not included other than as resources for human use – similar to the approach adopted by the contemporary theorist John Rawls (1999; see Kelly 2001; webpage: www.en.wikipedia.org/wiki/John_Rawls).

Today, the discourse on justice cannot escape the environmental and ecological dimensions. In fact, we increasingly see these as essential to justice making (see Conlon 1990; Primavesi 2003; 2004). From a geo-justice/eco-justice perspective, the Greek understanding is essentially bankrupt.

21. My concern in this chapter is to prioritise the humanity of Jesus, along lines promoted by increasing numbers of contemporary scholars (see Wink 2002). In no way should this be considered as a denial of the divinity of Jesus, a sophisticated theological interpretation best left to theologians. As an ordinary Christian, my hunch is that the divinity of Jesus is best accessed through his humanity (see O'Murchu 2005).

Bibliography

Abram, David (1996). *The Spell of the Sensuous*, New York: Vantage Books

Alexander, Donald (1990). 'Bioregionalism: Science or Sensibility', *Environmental Ethics*, 12 (2), 161–73

Arendt, Hannah (1999). *The Human Condition*, Chicago: University of Chicago Press

Avis, Paul (1989). *Eros and the Sacred*, London: SPCK

Bailie, Gil (1997). *Violence Unveiled*, New York: Crossroad

Barham, Penny (2003). 'Black Madonnas', *Feminist Theology*, 11, pp. 325–32

Begg, Ean (1996). *The Cult of the Black Virgin*, London: Penguin Books

Bell, Daniel M. (2001). *Liberation Theology and the End of History*, New York & London: Routledge

Berry, Thomas (1985). 'Bioregions: The Context for Reinhabiting the Earth', *Breakthrough*, Spring/Summer, 6–9

Black, Peter (2003). 'The Broken Wings of Eros: Christian Ethics and the Denial of Desire', *Theological Studies* 64, 106–26

Boff, Leonardo (1995). *Ecology and Liberation: A New Paradigm*, Maryknoll, NY: Orbis Books

Brock, Rita Nakishima, and Rebecca Ann Parker (2007). *Saving Paradise*, Boston: Beacon Press

Brueggemann, Walter (1978). *The Prophetic Imagination*, Minn.: Fortress Press

(1986). *The Hopeful Imagination*, Minn.: Fortress Press

(1993). *The Bible and Postmodern Imagination*, Minn.: Augsburg Fortress

Cannato, Judy (2006). *Radical Amazement*, Notre Dame, IN: Sorin Books

Carrette, Jeremy (2005). 'Intense Exchange: Sadomasochism, Theology and the Politics of Late Capitalism', *Theology & Sexuality*, 11, pp. 11–30

Carrette, Jeremy, and Richard King (2005). *Selling Spirituality: The Silent Takeover of Religion*, New York & London: Routledge

Casey, Edward (2000). *Remembering: A Phenomenological Study*, Bloomington, IN: Indiana University Press

Cavanaugh, William T. (1998). *Torture and Eucharist*, Malden Mass. Oxford: Blackwell

Chopra, Deepak (2000). *How to Know God*, New York: Harmony Books

(2004). *The Spontaneous Fulfilment of Desire*, CA: Three Rivers Press

Christ, Carol (1997). *Rebirth of the Goddess*, London: Routledge

Cobb, John (1991). *Matters of Life and Death*, Louisville, KY: Westminster/John

Knox Press

Cole, K.C. (2001). *The Hole in the Universe*, London & New York: Harcourt Inc.

Comblin, Jose (1998). *Called for Freedom: The Changing Context of Liberation Theology*, Maryknoll, NY: Orbis

Conforti, Michael (1999). *Field, Form and Fate: Patterns in Mind, Nature and Psyche*, Woodstock, Conn: Spring Publications Inc.

Conlon, James (1990). *Geo-Justice*, San Jose, CA: Resource Publications

(2004). *At the Edge of our Longing*, Ottawa: Novalis

Corbin, Henri (1972). 'Mundus Imaginalis: Or the Imaginary and the Imaginal', *Spring*, 1–19 (Dallas: Spring Publications)

(1998). *The Voyage and the Messenger*, Berkeley: North Atlantic Books

Crossan, John D. (1991). *The Historical Jesus*, New York: HarperCollins

(1994). *Jesus: A Revolutionary Biography*, San Francisco: HarperSanFrancisco

Cullinan, Cormac (2003). *Wild Law: A Manifesto for Earth Justice*, London: Green Books

Cupitt, Don (1998). *Mysticism after Modernity*, Oxford: Blackwell

Davies, Steven (1995). *Jesus the Healer*, London: SCM Press

Deleuze G., and F. Guattari (1983). *Anti-Oedipus: Capitalism and Schizophrenia*, Minn.: University of Minnesota Press

Dennett, Daniel (1992). *Consciousness Explained*, Newport Beach, CA: Back Bay Books

de Waal, Frans (1997). *Bonobo: The Forgotten Ape*, Los Angeles: University of California Press

(2005). *Our Inner Ape: The Best and Worst of Human Nature*, New York: Riverhead Books

Douglas-Klotz, Neil (1999). *The Hidden Gospel*, Wheaton, Ill.: Quest Books

Douthwaite, Richard (1998). *Short Circuit: Practical New Approach to Building more Self-Reliant Communities*, London: Green Books

Dreyer, Elizabeth A., and Mark S. Burrows, eds. (2005). *Minding the Spirit: The Study of Christian Spirituality*, Baltimore & London: The John Hopkins University Press

Dyer, Wayne (2004). *The Power of Intention*, London: Hay House Inc.

Edwards, Denis (1995). *Jesus the Wisdom of God: An Ecological Theology*, Maryknoll, NY: Orbis Books

(2004). *Breath of Life: A Theology of the Creator Spirit*, Maryknoll, NY: Orbis Books

Eisenberg, Evan (1998). *The Ecology of Eden: Humans, Nature and Human Nature*, New York: Alfred & Knoff

Eldredge, John (2000). *The Journey of Desire*, Nashville, TN: Thomas Nelson Publishers

Elias, Amy J. (2001). *Sublime Desire*, Baltimore: The John Hopkins University Press

Evola, Jules (1983). *The Metaphysics of Sex*, London: East-West Publications

Falk, Richard (2001). *Religion and Humane Global Governance*, New York: Pelgrave

Farley, Wendy (2005). *The Wounding and Healing of Desire*, Louisville, KY: WJK Press

Feuerbach, Ludwig (2004, initially 1845). *The Essence of Religion*, London: Prometheus Books

Flanagan, Bernadette, and David Kelly (2004). *Lamplighters: Exploring Spirituality in New Contexts*, Dublin: Veritas

Forman, Robert (2004). *Grassroots Spirituality*, Charlottesville, VA: Imprint Academic

Forrester, Duncan B. (1997). *Christian Justice and Public Policy*, Cambridge & New York: Cambridge University Press

Foucault, Michel (1977; 1985; 1986). *The History of Sexuality, Vol. 1 (The Will to Knowledge)*; *Vol. 2 (The Use of Pleasure)*; *Vol. 3 (The Care of the Self)*, New York: Viking

(1978). *The History of Sexuality: An Introduction*, New York: Random House

Fox, Matthew (1984). *Original Blessing: A Primer in Creation Spirituality*, Santa Fe: Bear & Co.

(1994). *The Re-invention of Work*, San Francisco: HarperSanFrancisco

(1999). *Sins of the Spirit, Blessings of the Flesh*, New York: Harmony Books

(2000). *One River, Many Wells*, New York: Jeremy P. Tarcher/Putnam

Frenier, Carol (2005). 'Engaging the Imaginal Realm: Doorway to Collective Wisdom', in www.collectivewisdominitiative.org

Fuery, Patrick (1995). *Theories of Desire*, Carlton, Vic.: Melbourne University Press

Gebara, Ivone (2002). *Out of the Depths: Women's Experience of Evil and Salvation*, Minn.: Fortress Press

Gebara, Ivone, and Maria Clara Bingemer (1989). *Guadalupe: Mother of the New Creation*, Maryknoll, NY: Orbis Books

Gebser, Jean (1986 – first printed in 1949). *The Ever-present Origin*, Athens, Ohio: Ohio University Press

Girard, René (1977). *Violence and the Sacred*, Baltimore: John Hopkins University Press

(1986). *The Scapegoat*, Baltimore: John Hopkins University Press

Goodall, Jane (2001). *My Life with Chimpanzees*, New York: Time Warner Audio Books

Goodchild, Veronica (2001). *Eros and Chaos: The Sacred Mysteries and Dark Shadows of Love*, York Beach, Maine: Nicholas-Hays Inc.

Grey, Mary C. (2003). *Sacred Longings: Ecofeminist Theology and Globalisation*, London: SCM Press

Harris, Maria (1997). *Dance of the Spirit*, New York: Bantam/Doubleday

Haught, John F. (1993). *Mystery and Promise: A Theology of Revelation*, Collegeville, Minn.: Liturgical Press

(2000). *God After Darwin*, Boulder, Col. & Oxford: Westview Press

(2003). *Deeper than Darwin*, Boulder, Col. & Oxford: Westview Press

Held, Virginia (2005). *The Ethics of Care: Personal, Political and Global*, Oxford: Oxford University Press

Henderson, Hazel (1988). *The Politics of the Solar Age*, New York: Anchor Books

Herzog, William (1994). *Parables as Subversive Speech*, Louisville, KY: WJK Press

(2004). *Prophet and Teacher: An Introduction to the Historical Jesus*, Louisville, KY: WJK Press

Heyward, Carter (1989). *Touching our Strength: The Erotic as Power and Love of God*, San Francisco: Harper

Hill, Jason (2000). *On Being a Cosmopolitan*, Lanham, MD & Oxford: Rowman & Littlefield

Hillman, James (1992). *Re-Visioning Psychology*, New York: HarperCollins

(2004a). *Archetypal Psychology*, Putnam, Conn.: Spring Publications

(2004b). *A Terrible Love of War*, New York & London: Penguin Books

Hines, Colin (2000). *Localisation: A Global Manifesto*, London: Earthscan Publications

Horgan, John (2003). *Rational Mysticism*, New York: Houghton Miffin Co.

Irigaray, Luce (1987). *Sexes and Genealogies*, New York: Columbia University Press.

Isherwood, Lisa (1999). *Liberating Christ*, Cleveland, OH: The Pilgrim Press

Johnson, Elizabeth (1992). *She Who Is*, New York: Crossroad

Johnston, William (2006). *Mystical Journey: An Autobiography*, Maryknoll, NY: Orbis Books

Jonas, Hans (1996). *Mortality and Morality*, Evanston, Ill: Northwestern University Press

Jordan, Mark (2000). *The Silence of Sodom: Homosexuality in Modern Catholicism*, Chicago: University of Chicago Press

Kadankavil, Thomas (1999). *Religion and Politics from Subaltern Perspective*, Bangalore: Dharmaram Publications

Keen, Sam (1985). *The Passionate Life*, London: Gateway Books

(1994). *Hymns to an Unknown God*, New York: Bantam Books

Kelly, Erin, ed. (2001). *Justice as Fairness: A Restatement*, Cambridge, Mass: Belknap Press

King, Joan C. (2004). *Cellular Wisdom*, Berkeley, CA & Toronto: Celestial Arts

Knitter, Paul F. (1995). *Jesus and the Other Names*, Maryknoll, NY: Orbis Books

Korten, David C. (2006). *The Great Turning: from Empire to Earth Community*, San Francisco: Berrett-Koehler

Kovel, Joel (1991). *History and Spirit*, Boston: Beacon Press

Kripal, John Jeffrey (2001). *Roads of Excess, Palaces of Wisdom: Eroticism and Reflexivity in the Study of Mysticism*, Chicago & London: University of Chicago Press

Leakey, Richard, and Roger Lewin (1996). *The Sixth Extinction: Biodiversity and its Survival*, London: Weidenfeld & Nicolson

Lewis, C.S. (1960). *The Four Loves*, New York: Harcourt Brace

Long, Stephen D. (2000). *Divine Economy: Theology and the Market*, New York: Routledge

Lorde, Audre (1989). *Sister Outsider: Essays and Speeches*, Berkeley: Crossing

Press, pp. 53–60

Loughlin, Gerard (2004). *Alien Sex: The Body and Desire in Cinema and Theology*, Oxford: Blackwell

Lovelock, James (1979). *Gaia: A New Look at Life on Earth*, New York: Oxford University Press

(1988). *The Ages of Gaia*, New York: Oxford University Press

McFague, Sallie (1997). *Super, Natural Christians*, Minn.: Augsburg Fortress; London: SCM Press

(2001). *Life Abundant*, Minn.: Fortress Press

McGinn, Bernard (1994). *The Foundations of Mysticism* (Vol. 1), New York: Herder & Herder

McIntosh, Marc (1998). *Mystical Theology*, Oxford: Blackwell

McTaggart, Lynne (2001). *The Field: The Quest for the Secret Force of the Universe*, London: Thorsons/HarperCollins

Manktelow, Alan (2005). 'Some Thoughts on the Art of Our Time', *Human Givens*, 12/2 (2005), 21–3

Mann, A. T., and Jane Lyle (1995). *Sacred Sexuality*, Shaftsbury, Dorset & Rockport, Mass.: Element Books

Manning, Richard (2004). *Against the Grain: How Agriculture has Hijacked Civilisation*, New York: North Point Press

Margulis, Lynn (in conjunction with Dorian Sagan) (1995). *What is Life?* London: Weidenfeld & Nicolson

(1998). *The Symbiotic Planet: A New Look at Evolution*, New York: Basic Books

Mithen, Steven (2005). *The Singing Neanderthals*, London: Weidenfeld & Nicolson

Moore, Thomas (1992). *Care of the Soul*, San Francisco: Harper

(1994). *Soulmates*, San Francisco: Harper

(1998). *The Soul of Sex*, New York: HarperCollins

(2004). *Dark Nights of the Soul*, London: Piatkus Books

Nadeau, Robert, and Menas Kafatos (1999). *The Non-Local Universe*, New York & Oxford: Oxford University Press

Nichols, Terence (2003). *The Sacred Cosmos*, Grand Rapids, MI: Brazos Press

Nygren, Anders (1969). *Agape and Eros*, New York: Harper & Row

O'Donohue, John (1997). *Anam Chara*, New York: Bantam Press

(2003). *Divine Beauty: The Invisible Embrace*, London: Bantam Books

O'Murchu, Diarmuid (1997). *Reclaiming Spirituality*, New York: Crossroad

(2000). *Religion in Exile*, New York: Crossroad

(2002). *Evolutionary Faith*, Maryknoll, NY: Orbis Books

(2004). *Quantum Theology*, revised edition, New York: Crossroad

(2005). *Catching Up with Jesus*, New York: Crossroad

O'Sullivan, Edmund (ed) (2002). *Expanding the Boundaries of Transformative Learning*, New York: Palgrave

Page, Ruth (1996). *God and the Web of Creation*, London: SCM Press

Phillips, Jan (2006). *The art of original thinking*, San Diego, CA: 9th Element Press

Plumwood, Val (2002). *Environmental Culture: The Ecological Crisis of Reason*, New York & London: Routledge

Polak, Fred (1973). *The Image of the Future*, Burlington, Mass.: Elsevier Scientific Publishing

Primavesi, Anne (2003). *Gaia's Gift*, New York & London: Routledge

(2004). *Making God Laugh*, Santa Rosa, CA: Polebridge Press

Raine, Kathleen (1991). *Autobiographies*, London: Skoob Seriph

Rawls, John (1999). *A Theory of Justice*, Oxford: Oxford University Press (initially published in 1971)

Ray, Darby Kathleen (1998). *Deceiving the Devil: Atonement, Abuse and Ransom*, Cleveland, OH: The Pilgrim Press

Ricoeur, Paul (1964). 'Wonder, Eroticism and Enigma', *Cross Currents* 14, pp. 133–141

Ritzer, George (2004). *The Globalization of Nothing*, London: Sage Publications Inc.

Roszak, Theodore (1978). *Person/Planet*, New York: Doubleday/Anchor

Ruether, Rosemary Radford (2005). *Goddesses and the Divine Feminine*, Berkeley: University of California Press

Sahtouris, Elizabet (1998). *EarthDance: Living Systems in Evolution*, Alameda, CA: Metalog Books

Sale, Kirkpatrick (1991). *Dwellers in the Land*, San Francisco: Sierra Club

Schroeder, Timothy (2004). *Three Faces of Desire*, Oxford & New York: Oxford University Press

Schussler Fiorenza, Elizabeth (1983). *In Memory of Her*, London: SCM Press

Soelle, Dorothee (2001). *The Silent Cry: Mysticism and Resistance*, Minn: Augsburg/Fortress

Stewart, John (2000). *Evolution's Arrow*, Canberra (Aus): Chapman Press

Suchocki, Marjorie Hewitt (1999). *The Fall to Violence*, New York: Continuum

Suzuki, David (2002). *The Sacred Balance: Rediscovering our place in nature*, Vancouver: Douglas & McIntyre Ltd

Swimme, Brian, and Thomas Berry (1992). *The Universe Story*, San Francisco: Harper

Sylvester, Nancy, and Mary Jo Klick, eds. (2004). *Crucible for Change*, Boerne, TX: Sor Juana Press

Tacey, David (2004). *The Spiritual Revolution* (Australia): Brunner Routledge

Turner, Denys (1995a). *The Darkness of God: Negativity in Christian Mysticism*, Cambridge, UK: Cambridge University Press

(1995b). *Eros and Allegory: Medieval Exegesis of the Song of Songs*, Kalamazoo, Mich.: Cistercian Publications

Turney, Jon (2003). *Lovelock and Gaia: Signs of Life*, Cambridge, UK: Icon Books Ltd

Underhill, Evelyn (1911). *Mysticism*, London: Methuen (repr. London: Bracken Books, 1995)

Van Ness, Peter (1992). *Spirituality, Diversion and Decadence*, Albany NY: State University of New York Press

Vance, Carole S. (1984). *Pleasure and Danger: Exploring Female Sexuality*, London: Routledge

Walker, Margaret Urban (1997). *Moral Understandings: A Feminist Study in Ethics*, London & New York: Routledge

Wallace, Mark I. (2002). *Fragments of the Spirit*, Harrisburg, Penn.: Trinity Press International

(2005). *Finding God in the Singing River*, Minneapolis: Fortress Press

Weeks, Jeffrey (1985). *Sexuality and its Discontents*, New York: Routledge & Kegan Paul

(1986). *Sexuality*, London: Routledge

(1991). *Against Nature: History, Sexuality and Identity*, London: Rivers Oram Press

Wheatley, Margaret J. (1992). *Leadership and the New Science*, San Francisco: Berrett-Koehler

Whyte, David (2001). *Crossing the Unknown Sea*, New York: Riverhead Books

Wilshire, Bruce (1998). *Wild Hunger: The Primal Roots of Modern Addiction*, Lanham, MD & Oxford: Rowman & Littlefield

Wink, Walter (2002). *The Human Being: Jesus and the Enigma of the Son of Man*, Minn.: Fortress Press

Zweig, Connie (2003). *The Holy Longing: The Hidden Power of Spiritual Yearning*, New York: Jeremy P. Tarcher

Index